T0146354

Exploring the Feasibility and Utility of
Machine Learning-Assisted Command and Control

Volume 1, Findings and Recommendations

MATTHEW WALSH, LANCE MENTHE, EDWARD GEIST,
ERIC HASTINGS, JOSHUA KERRIGAN, JASMIN LÉVEILLÉ,
JOSHUA MARGOLIS, NICHOLAS MARTIN, BRIAN P. DONNELLY

Prepared for the Department of the Air Force
Approved for public release; distribution unlimited

RAND PROJECT AIR FORCE

For more information on this publication, visit **www.rand.org/t/RRA263-1**.

About RAND

The RAND Corporation is a research organization that develops solutions to public policy challenges to help make communities throughout the world safer and more secure, healthier and more prosperous. RAND is nonprofit, nonpartisan, and committed to the public interest. To learn more about RAND, visit www.rand.org.

Research Integrity

Our mission to help improve policy and decisionmaking through research and analysis is enabled through our core values of quality and objectivity and our unwavering commitment to the highest level of integrity and ethical behavior. To help ensure our research and analysis are rigorous, objective, and nonpartisan, we subject our research publications to a robust and exacting quality-assurance process; avoid both the appearance and reality of financial and other conflicts of interest through staff training, project screening, and a policy of mandatory disclosure; and pursue transparency in our research engagements through our commitment to the open publication of our research findings and recommendations, disclosure of the source of funding of published research, and policies to ensure intellectual independence. For more information, visit www.rand.org/about/principles.

RAND's publications do not necessarily reflect the opinions of its research clients and sponsors.

Published by the RAND Corporation, Santa Monica, Calif.
© 2021 RAND Corporation
RAND® is a registered trademark.

Library of Congress Cataloging-in-Publication Data is available for this publication.

ISBN: 978-1-9774-0709-2

Cover: U.S. Air Force photo; MF3d/Getty Images.

Preface

Recent high-profile demonstrations of artificial intelligence (AI) systems achieving superhuman performance on increasingly complex games along with successful commercial applications of related technology raise the questions of whether and how the U.S. Air Force can use AI for military planning and command and control (C2). The potential benefits of applying AI to C2 include greater decision speed, increased capacity to deal with the heterogeneity and volume of data, enhanced planning and execution dynamism, improved ability to synchronize multimodal effects, and more efficient use of human capital. Together, the technology push prompted by recent breakthroughs in AI and the market pull arising from emerging C2 needs have prompted the Air Force and the Department of Defense to identify AI as a strategic asset.

In 2019, the Air Force Research Laboratory, Information Directorate (AFRL/RI) asked RAND Project AIR FORCE (PAF) to examine and recommend opportunities for applying AI to Air Force C2. The research project Exploring the Near-Term Feasibility and Utility of Machine Learning-Assisted Operational Planning was conducted in PAF's Force Modernization program to address this question. A second project was conducted in parallel to examine the separate but related topic of complexity imposition. This report presents the primary result of the study on AI: an analytical framework for understanding the suitability of a particular AI system for a given C2 problem and for evaluating the AI system when applied to the problem. We demonstrate the analytical framework with three technical case studies focused on master air attack planning, sensor management, and personnel recovery.

The C2 processes examined in these case studies are central to current and future C2 concepts of operation, and they exemplify the range of characteristics that make C2 problems so challenging.

RAND Project AIR FORCE

RAND Project AIR FORCE (PAF), a division of the RAND Corporation, is the Department of the Air Force's (DAF's) federally funded research and development center for studies and analyses, supporting both the United States Air Force and the United States Space Force. PAF provides DAF with independent analyses of policy alternatives affecting the development, employment, combat readiness, and support of current and future air, space, and cyber forces. Research is conducted in four programs: Strategy and Doctrine; Force Modernization and Employment; Manpower, Personnel, and Training; and Resource Management. The research reported here was prepared under contract FA7014-16-D-1000.

Additional information about PAF is available on our website: www.rand.org/paf/

This report documents work originally shared with DAF on March 11, 2020. The draft report, issued on April 14, 2020, was reviewed by formal peer reviewers and DAF subject-matter experts.

Contents

Figures and Tables

Figures

Tables

Summary

Issues

- A key priority for the U.S. Air Force is to use artificial intelligence (AI) to enhance military command and control (C2).
- The academic and commercial contexts in which AI systems have been developed and deployed are qualitatively different from the military contexts in which they are needed.
- The Air Force lacks an analytical framework for understanding the suitability of different AI systems for different C2 problems and for identifying pervasive technology gaps.
- The Air Force lacks sufficient metrics of merit for evaluating the performance, effectiveness, and suitability of AI systems for C2 problems.

Approach

The RAND team reviewed the computer science, cognitive science, and operations research literature to create a taxonomy of C2 problem characteristics and a taxonomy of AI solution capabilities. These taxonomies were refined through interviews with military C2 subject-matter experts and with experts in AI. To determine the solution capabilities essential for dealing with each problem characteristic, the RAND team conducted an online expert panel. Finally, the RAND team demonstrated the framework for evaluating the suitability of different AI systems for C2 problems through three technical case studies developed in conjunction with active-duty and retired AF personnel.

Conclusions and Recommendations

The RAND team proposes a structured method for determining the suitability of an AI system for any given C2 process (Figure S.1). The methodology involves (1) evaluating the C2 problem characteristics, (2) evaluating the AI system capabilities, (3) comparing alignment between problem characteristics and solution capabilities, (4) selecting measures of merit, and (5) implementing, testing, and evaluating potential AI systems. In addition to providing a methodology to determine alignment between C2 problems and AI solutions, this research supports several conclusions shown in Figure S.1 along with associated recommendations.

Conclusion 1. C2 processes are very different from games and environments used to develop and demonstrate AI systems.

- *Recommendation 1.* Use the structured method described in this report to systematically analyze the characteristics of games, problems, and C2 processes to determine where existing AI test beds are representative and nonrepresentative of C2 tasks.

Figure S.1
Artificial Intelligence System Capability Mapping and Command and Control Process Evaluation

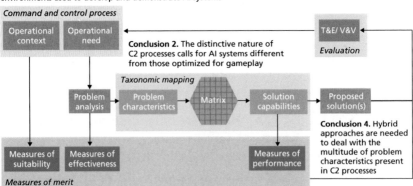

Conclusion 1. C2 processes are very different from many of the games and environments used to develop and demonstrate AI systems

Command and control process

Operational context

Operational need

Conclusion 2. The distinctive nature of C2 processes calls for AI systems different from those optimized for gameplay

T&E/ V&V

Evaluation

Taxonomic mapping

Problem analysis

Problem characteristics

Matrix

Solution capabilities

Proposed solution(s)

Conclusion 4. Hybrid approaches are needed to deal with the multitude of problem characteristics present in C2 processes

Measures of suitability

Measures of effectiveness

Measures of performance

Measures of merit

Conclusion 3. New guidance, infrastructure, and metrics are needed to evaluate applications of AI to C2

NOTE: T&E: test and evaluation; V&V: verification and validation.

- *Recommendation 2.* Develop new AI test beds that are more representative of C2 tasks.

Conclusion 2. The distinctive nature of C2 processes calls for AI systems different from those optimized for game play.

- *Recommendation 3.* Use the structured method described in this report to identify and invest in high-priority solution capabilities called for across a wide range of C2 processes and not currently available (e.g., *robustness* and *assuredness*).
- *Recommendation 4.* Use the structured method described in this report to evaluate alignment between the characteristics of potential AI systems and particular C2 processes to prioritize which systems to develop.

Conclusion 3. The distinctive nature of C2 processes calls for measures of merit different from those typically used in AI research.

- *Recommendation 5.* Develop metrics for AI solutions that assess capabilities beyond algorithm soundness and optimality.
- *Recommendation 6.* Use the structured method described in this report to identify key measures of performance, effectiveness, and suitability for a given C2 process and to comprehensively assess candidate AI solutions.

Conclusion 4. Hybrid approaches are needed to deal with the multitude of problem characteristics present in C2 processes.

- *Recommendation 7.* Identify, reuse, and combine algorithmic solutions that confer critical AI system capabilities.

Acknowledgments

We would like to thank our sponsor, Jack Blackhurst (Air Force Research Laboratory executive director), and our action officers, Nate Gemelli and Lee Seversky (AFRL/RI), for their help in shaping and performing this report. We would also like to thank Mark Linderman, Julie Brichacek, and Rick Metzger (AFRL/RI) for their valuable input during the study.

We are deeply appreciative of the assistance with data collection we received from many personnel, including Lt Col Dennis Borrman (2020 RAND Air Force Fellows Program), Lt Col Jason Chambers (2020 RAND Air Force Fellows Program), LTC David Spencer (2020 RAND Arroyo Army Fellows Program), and MAJ Ian Fleischmann (2020 RAND Arroyo Army Fellows Program). We are also appreciative of the time that so many analysts and other personnel dedicated to participating in the expert panel.

Finally, we thank the many RAND colleagues who helped us with this work. Principally, but not exclusively, we thank Brien Alkire, Michael Bohnert, Jim Chow, Rick Garvey, Henry Hargrove, Dmitry Khodyakov, Osonde Osoba, Libby May, Yuliya Shokh, and Abbie Tingstad.

Abbreviations

AFRL/RI   Air Force Research Laboratory, Information Directorate

AI   artificial intelligence

AOC   Air Operations Center

ATC   air tasking cycle

C2   command and control

DARPA   Defense Advanced Research Projects Agency

DIB   Defense Innovation Board

DoD   Department of Defense

ISR   Intelligence, Surveillance, and Reconnaissance

JADC2   Joint All-Domain Command and Control

MAAP   master air attack plan

MIP   mixed integer program

ML   machine learning

MoE   measures of effectiveness

MoP   Measures of Performance

MoS   Measures of Suitability

OODA   observe, orient, decide, and act

PAF	Project AIR FORCE
T&E	Test and Evaluation
TLAM	Tomahawk Land Attack Missile
TRD	Technical Requirements Document
V&V	Verification and Validation
WS	weapon system

Introduction and Project Overview

In November 2014, former Secretary of Defense Chuck Hagel articulated a Third Offset Strategy, which focused on robotics, autonomous systems, and data.[1] The strategy echoed recommendations from earlier science and technology reports by the Department of Defense (DoD), the armed forces, and other federal agencies. For example, of the 30 potential capability areas called out for emphasis by the U.S. Air Force in *Technology Horizons: A Vision for Air Force Science and Technology 2010–2030*, "adaptive flexibly-autonomous systems" was given highest priority.[2] More recently, the 2019 National Defense Authorization Act established the Joint AI Center to coordinate DoD's efforts to develop and transition artificial intelligence (AI) technologies and also a National Security Commission on Artificial Intelligence to ensure national leadership in the development of AI technologies.[3] These legislative actions have been accompanied by increased funding: in 2018, for example, the Defense Advanced Research Projects Agency (DARPA) announced a $2 billion campaign for AI technology development.[4]

---

[1] DoD, "Secretary of Defense Speech, Reagan National Defense Forum Keynote," Defense .gov, December 7, 2019. DoD lacks agreed upon definitions of *autonomy* and of *artificial intelligence*. Although the two terms are not synonymous, any autonomous system contains one or more forms of AI.

[2] W. J. Dahm, *Technology Horizons: A Vision for Air Force Science and Technology During 2010–2030*, Arlington, Va.: U.S. Air Force, 2010.

[3] Sections 238 and 1051 of the National Defense Authorization Act, respectively.

[4] DARPA, "DARPA Announces $2 Billion Campaign to Develop Next Wave of AI Technologies," Arlington, Va., March 12, 2020.

Breakthroughs in computing power, data availability, and algorithms during the past fifteen years have contributed to a surge of interest. Demonstrations of AI systems achieving superhuman performance on complex games like chess, poker, and *StarCraft* reveal their ever-increasing capabilities. Additionally, commercial applications of AI systems have overwhelmingly established their real-world value.[5] Despite the abstraction from military contexts, DoD has frequently cited potential applications of these technologies to warfighting functions.[6] China and Russia have also undertaken extensive programs in AI, giving urgency to the United States' pursuit of these technologies to maintain a strategic advantage.[7]

DoD's recent interest in AI is also driven by emerging needs.[8] For example, the proliferation of wide-area surveillance sensor systems gives rise to volumes of data that exceed human processing capacity. Additionally, the imposition of joint all-domain effects requires planning and coordinating across a suite of capabilities that challenges human ability to manage complexity. Lastly, improvements in unmanned platforms and the need to operate in contested environments places vehicles beyond the range of human control. Yet despite the apparent potential for AI to address these and other challenges, it remains difficult to discern the applicability of specific academic and commercial AI systems to specific warfighting functions.

---

[5] For example, see Bernard Marr and Matt Ward, *Artificial Intelligence in Practice: How 50 Successful Companies Used AI and Machine Learning to Solve Problems*, Chichester, U.K.: Wiley, 2019.

[6] U.S. Air Force Scientific Advisory Board, *Technologies for Enabling Resilient Command and Control MDC2 Overview*, Washington, D.C., 2018; G. Zacharias, *Autonomous Horizons: The Way Forward*, Maxwell Air Force Base, Ala.: Air University Press, Curtis E. LeMay Center for Doctrine Development and Education, 2019a.

[7] This has been reported extensively elsewhere. For example, see Yuna Huh Wong, John M. Yurchak, Robert W. Button, Aaron Frank, Burgess Laird, Osonde A. Osoba, Randall Steeb, Benjamin N. Harris, and Sebastian Joon Bae, *Deterrence in the Age of Thinking Machines*, Santa Monica, Calif.: RAND Corporation, RR-2797-RC, 2020.

[8] U.S. Air Force, *Science and Technology Strategy: Strengthening USAF Science and Technology for 2030 and Beyond*, Washington, D.C., April 2019b.

This report concerns the potential for AI systems to assist in Air Force command and control (C2) from a technical perspective. Specifically, we present an analytical framework for assessing the suitability of a given AI system for a given C2 problem. The purpose of the framework is to identify AI systems that address the distinct needs of different C2 problems and to identify the technical gaps that remain.[9] Although we focus on C2, the analytical framework applies to other warfighting functions and services as well.

Study Context

Terminology

For the purposes of this report, we define AI and machine learning (ML) as follows: AI is an academic discipline concerned with machines demonstrating intelligence—that is, behaving in a rational way given what they know;[10] ML is a subfield of AI that concerns machines performing tasks without first receiving explicit instructions. The field of AI is expansive and includes topics such as problem-solving, knowledge and reasoning, planning, and learning. ML is a type of AI in which the machine learns to perform tasks through exposure to training data or through interactions with a simulation environment. Neural networks are but one class of ML techniques, along with many other statistical methods.

The Need for Artificial Intelligence in Command and Control

C2 is "the exercise of authority and direction by a properly designated commander over assigned and attached forces in the accomplishment

---

[9] Though important, we do not address other operational, doctrinal, and organizational issues surrounding the use of AI in this report. Defense Science Board, *Defense Science Board Summer Study on Autonomy*, Washington, D.C.: Office of the Under Secretary of Defense, June 2016; U.S. Air Force, *Artificial Intelligence Annex to the Department of Defense Artificial Intelligence Strategy*, Washington, D.C., 2019a.

[10] S. Russell and P. Norvig, *Introduction to Artificial Intelligence: A Modern Approach*, New Delhi: Prentice-Hall of India, 1995.

of the mission."[11] The goal of C2 is to enable what is otherwise operationally possible by planning, synchronizing, and integrating forces in time and purpose. AI systems have the potential to address immediate, midterm, and far-term C2 needs.

Immediate needs. The Air Operations Center (AOC) provides operational-level C2 of air and space forces to accomplish joint force commander objectives. The AOC Technical Requirements Document contains more than 700 technical requirements traceable to operational requirements and to the AOC mission threads.[12] Presently, mission threads are supported by a patchwork of legacy software systems, and the tasks they entail are immensely human intensive. The AOC development and modernization outlined in the AOC 10.2 program sought to address these challenges in part by facilitating task flows through increased automation.

The AOC technical requirements fall into two general categories: those that involve modifying information objects, such as creating a master air attack plan based on the commander's guidance and other inputs, and those that involve simply storing or handling information objects, such as publishing the air tasking order and transmitting it to units. Requirements in the former category, which account for 44 percent of total requirements, are more likely to call for AI because they involve reasoning about inputs to reach decisions. Figure 1.1 shows the number of requirements by type and mission thread. Opportunities for AI are ubiquitous across mission threads and throughout the air tasking cycle (ATC). The AOC 10.2 program called for increasingly autonomous capabilities like "automated airspace deconfliction" and

---

[11] Joint Publication 3-0, *Joint Operations*, Washington, D.C.: U.S. Joint Chiefs of Staff, January 17, 2017. Command is the authority lawfully exercised over subordinates, and control is the process—inherent in command—by which commanders plan, guide, and conduct operations.

[12] Lockheed Martin Information Systems and Global Services, *Technical Requirements Document (TRD), for the Air and Space Operations Center (AOC) Weapon System (WS)*, draft, AOCWS-TRD-0000-U-R8C0, prepared for 652 ELSS/KQ Electronic Systems Center, Hanscom AFB, Colorado Springs, Colo.: Lockheed Martin Information Systems and Global Services, November 16, 2009. Not available to the general public.

Figure 1.1
Number of Requirements by Type and by Air Operations Center Mission Thread

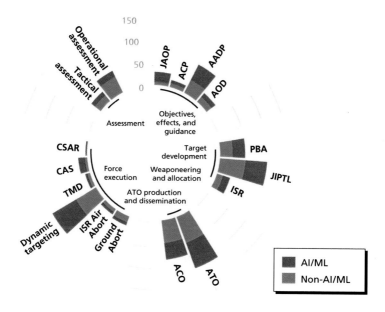

SOURCE: Lockheed Martin Information Systems and Global Services, Technical Requirements Document (TRD), for the Air and Space Operations Center (AOC) Weapon System (WS), draft, AOCWS-TRD-0000-U-R8C0, prepared for 652 ELSS/KQ Electronic Systems Center, Hanscom AFB, Colorado Springs, Colo.: Lockheed Martin Information Systems and Global Services, November 16, 2009.

NOTE: ACO: Airspace Control Order Development; ACP: Airspace Control Plan; AADP: Area Air Defense Plan; AOD: Air Operations Directive; ATO (air tasking order): ATO Development; CAS: Close Air Support; CSAR: Combat Search and Rescue; DT: Dynamic Targeting; ISR (intelligence, surveillance, and reconnaissance): ISR Planning; JAOP: Joint Air Operations Planning; JIPTL: Joint Integrated Prioritized List Development; PBA: Predictive Battlespace Awareness; TMD: Theater Missile Defense.

"smart agent decision aids." Following the cancelation of the AOC 10.2 in 2016, these capabilities have not yet been delivered.

The retirement of legacy the AOC systems and the deployment of new Block 20 applications by Kessel Run provide an on-ramp for AI into operational-level C2. Additionally, the enterprise services and platform managed by Kessel Run enable the transition of software— potentially including AI—to the AOC. Finally, other Kessel Run products in development, such as Rebel Alliance, enable automatic data sharing across the AOC, creating new opportunities for AI.

Midterm needs. The ATC is the canonical 72-hour process used for the planning, execution, monitoring, and evaluation of air power. Yet Cold War–era assumptions that once motivated the ATC fail to meet the dynamics needed for defensive operations and real-time mission changes.[13] During Operation Desert Storm, 20 to 40 percent of sorties changed from conception to execution. During Operation Allied Force, the emphasis on fielded forces gave rise to flex targeting, which matured into dynamic targeting. During Operation Enduring Freedom, most fixed targets were destroyed within the first 15 minutes of the war. Finally, during Operation Iraqi Freedom, kill-box interdiction and close air support accounted for 79 percent of designated mean points of impact struck, and dynamic targeting and time sensitive targeting accounted for an additional 4 percent of designated mean points of impact struck.

These examples show that the majority of missions in recent conflicts were planned outside the ATC. Although extensive manual replanning was feasible in these cases, it would likely be infeasible in a conflict with a near peer that involved substantial resource limitations and for which air superiority was not assured. AI could enable more dynamic planning by dramatically shortening the duration of the ATC, by accounting for more contingencies during the deliberate planning phase, and by developing and enacting new contingencies during force execution. The need for AI to facilitate planning will increase as the Air Force adopts Joint All-Domain Command and Control (JADC2) due to the greater diversity of available effects and, hence, the complexity of coordinating them.

Far-term needs. "Centralized control and decentralized execution" are long-standing tenets of air power.[14] Yet the concentration of operational planning processes and staffs at forward deployed AOCs con-

---

[13] Robert Winkler, *The Evolution of the Joint ATO Cycle*, Norfolk, Va.: Joint Advanced Warfighting School, 2006.

[14] Joint Publication 3-30, *Command and Control of Joint Air Operations*, Washington, D.C.: U.S. Joint Chiefs of Staff, January 12, 2010.

stitutes a critical vulnerability. One way to increase the resiliency of air component C2 is to evolve from the current centralized C2 architecture to a globally distributed one. However, this requires that the architecture be robust against disrupted communications and the temporary or permanent loss of nodes.[15] AI could enable distributed C2 by prioritizing communications between nodes, by coordinating planning activities across intermittently isolated nodes, and by allowing smaller and potentially less experienced staffs to complete planning activities. The need for AI to coordinate activities will increase as the Air Force adopts JADC2, which is inherently dispersed across geographically and functionally dispersed nodes.

Potential use cases for AI in the Air Force and DoD are not limited to C2. For example, the first two National Mission Initiatives identified by the Joint AI Center involve using computer vision to extract information from imagery (e.g., Project Maven) and predictive vehicle maintenance to increase readiness by pre-positioning parts and maintenance personnel.[16] AI could also be applied to Air Force training and professional education (e.g., Pilot Training Next). Although we primarily focus on C2, there are potential applications for AI across all Air Staff directorates.

Recent Technological Advances in Artificial Intelligence

Since the advent of AI, human games have served as a benchmark for evaluating computer intelligence.[17] Many recent high-profile demonstrations have shown AI systems achieving superhuman performance on increasingly difficult games of strategy and skill. At one time, each of the games listed in Table 1.1 was thought to require uniquely human abilities. For example, the game of go has been described as one of the "most challenging domains in terms of human intellect," a view that

---

[15] U.S. Air Force Scientific Advisory Board, 2018.

[16] John Shanahan, "Artificial Intelligence Initiatives," statement to the Senate Armed Services Committee Subcommittee on Emerging Threats and Capabilities, Washington, D.C., U.S. Senate, March 12, 2019.

[17] N. Ensmenger, "Is Chess the Drosophila of Artificial Intelligence? A Social History of an Algorithm," *Social Studies of Science*, Vol. 42, No. 1, 2012.

Table 1.1
Recent Milestones in Artificial Intelligence Game Play

Source	Game	Key Characteristics	System Architecture
Mnih et al., 2013	Atari games	Continuous play High dimensionality	Deep reinforcement learning
Silver et al., 2018	Go, chess, *shogi* (Japanese chess)	High dimensionality	Deep reinforcement learning Monte Carlo tree search
Brown and Sandholm, 2018	No-limit Texas hold'em	High dimensionality Imperfect information	Monte Carlo counterfactual regret minimization Subgame solving Self-improvement
Vinyals et al., 2019	*StarCraft II*	Continuous play High dimensionality Imperfect information Multiplayer	Deep reinforcement learning

has motivated over 50 years of AI research on games of the mind.[18] Indeed, many of these games have been used by cognitive scientists to study human memory, planning, and expertise.[19] The finding that AI systems can outperform elite-level humans in these games is, then, somewhat remarkable and suggests that AI may be relevant for tasks once thought to require human cognition.[20]

Recent commercial applications of AI systems have been equally impressive (Table 1.2). Neural networks have been trained to achieve cardiologist-level performance at classifying electrocardiogram readings; optimization techniques have been used to control energy plant

---

[18] David Silver, Thomas Hubert, Julian Schrittwieser, Ioannis Antonoglou, Matthew Lai, Arthur Guez, Marc Lanctot, Laurent Sifre, Dharshan Kumaran, Thore Graepel, Timothy Lillicrap, Karen Simonyan, and Demis Hassabi, "A General Reinforcement Learning Algorithm that Masters Chess, Shogi, and Go Through Self-Play," *Science*, Vol. 362, No. 6419, December 2018.

[19] F. Gobet and H. A. Simon, "Templates in Chess Memory: A Mechanism for Recalling Several Boards," *Cognitive Psychology*, Vol. 31, No. 1, 1996.

[20] In some games, such as chess, *advanced play* by teams of expert humans and computer programs has been explored, although the strongest players are now purely computational.

Table 1.2
Recent Milestones in Applied Artificial Intelligence

Source	Task	System Architecture
Hannun et al., 2019	Detect irregularities in continuous electrocardiogram leads	Neural network trained using supervised learning paradigm to identify 12 rhythm classes from 91K (labeled) electrocardiogram lead samples
Jamei et al., 2019	Determine best operating levels for electric power plants to meet demands throughout transmission network	Neural network trained to provide a warm start to IPOPT optimization method
Julian, Kochenderfer, and Owen, 2019	Airborne collision avoidance threat detection and escape maneuver selection	Train deep neural network to compress and approximate state-action lookup table
Sinha et al., 2018	Generate U.S. Coast Guard patrol schedules for port of Boston and park ranger patrols for wildlife protection	Quantile response model of attacker embedded in Stackelberg game

production and transmission; game theory approaches have been used for patrol scheduling by the U.S. Coast Guard in the port of Boston.[21] These examples underscore that AI is no longer a mere academic curiosity but offers real-world value. Additionally, they show that AI systems can function successfully as components of larger human-machine teams.

Managing Artificial Intelligence Expectations

Amid the recent hype surrounding AI, it is important to remember that DoD not only has been investing in AI research since the 1950s but was the primary funder of AI research through the early 2000s.[22]

---

[21] The DoD defense industrial base is also advancing applied AI in such areas as processing, exploitation, and dissemination (e.g., Project Maven), operational C2 (e.g., DARPA Resilient Synchronized Planning and Assessment for the Contested Environment), and tactical control (e.g., DARPA Air Combat Evolution).

[22] National Research Council, *Funding a Revolution: Government Support for Computing Research*, Washington, D.C.: National Academy Press, 1999.

During the past 70 years, and across the first and second AI "winters,"[23] the Advanced Research Projects Agency and DARPA have provided continuous support for basic and applied AI research. This support has contributed to various commercial successes. For example, the multibillion-dollar market for autonomous cars can be traced back to the first DARPA Grand Challenge; and Siri emerged from the DARPA Personal Assistant that Learns program. This support has also contributed to various military successes. For example, U.S. Transportation Command used the Dynamic Analysis and Replanning Tool during Operation Desert Storm to move tanks and heavy artillery to Saudi Arabia three weeks faster than would have otherwise been possible, and the Command Post of the Future has become a U.S. Army program of record.

Notwithstanding these successes, few AI systems have been transitioned to the military. To enable such transitions, the right technological capabilities must be aligned to operational needs and integrated with existing and emerging systems. The following four issues encompass some of the primary challenges to this transition:

- *Issue 1: alignment with operational needs.* The lack of AI expertise embedded within the Air Force, paired with the sensitive nature of operational planning and execution tasks, makes it hard to assess alignment between AI systems and military tasks. Understanding the former requires depth of computer science knowledge; understanding the latter requires depth of operational knowledge. Complicating matters, the operational needs associated with nascent JADC2 concepts of operations are ill defined.
- *Issue 2: remaining technology gaps.* DoD needs are not perfectly aligned with commercial demand signals. For example, many DoD problems lack large labeled-data sets. Additionally, they lack high-speed, high-fidelity simulation environments. Finally, they require stronger assurances because of their consequential nature. DoD must take an active role in promoting the development of critical technologies not already being strongly addressed by the

---

[23] For example, see Kathleen Walch, "Are We Heading for Another AI Winter Soon?," *Forbes*, October 20, 2019.

industry (e.g., data-efficient learning, transfer learning, and verification and validation [V&V]).

- *Issue 3: integration with existing systems.* The AOC comprises more than 50 commercial and government off-the-shelf technologies and third-party applications.[24] The applications and interfaces they share are proprietary and frequently modified. The challenge of integrating the patchwork legacy C2 structure that makes up the AOC was one factor that contributed to the cancelation of the AOC 10.2.[25]
- *Issue 4: integration with emerging capabilities.* The AOC is but one of many C2 nodes. Ultimately, AI must also be integrated with all domain distributed planning cells (i.e., space and cyber), multiservice systems (e.g., Distributed Common Ground System and Advanced Battle Management System), and tactical platforms. Like the AOC, the technical architectures associated with each are constantly evolving.

In this report, we primarily focus on determining alignment between AI systems and C2 processes (Issue 1). Our analysis of C2 processes is also informative with respect to pervasive technological capabilities that will be required of DoD AI systems (Issue 2). Finally, the metrics we identify for evaluating DoD AI systems include system integration (Issues 3 and 4).

Study Methodology

As AI moves out of the laboratory and into the home, workplace, and battle space, the need to identify high-quality solutions to real-world problems grows ever more acute. Applied AI demands methodologies

---

[24] Air Force Life Cycle Management Center, Battle Management Directorate, *Descriptive List of Applicable Publications (DLOAP) for the Air Operations Center (AOC)*, Hanscom Air Force Base, Mass., April 1, 2019. Not available to the general public.

[25] DoD, *A Critical Change to the Air Operations Center—Weapon System Increment 10.2 Program Increased Costs and Delayed Deployment for 3 Years*, Washington, D.C.: Inspector General, DODIG-2017-079, 2017a.

to identify promising solutions for practical use cases. We conducted a literature review of existing frameworks. We synthesized characteristics of existing frameworks and tailored them to the unique characteristics of C2 and other military problems. In this section we present the resulting framework.

The methodology we developed comprises two complementary taxonomies for problem and solution characteristics. The two taxonomies each begins with a small number of broad categories, which then branch out into a larger number of subcategories. The subcategories of the two respective taxonomies converge to identify probable value criteria. As a key fits a lock, the AI system's capabilities must be aligned with the problem's characteristic (Figure 1.2). For example, a problem with a dearth of data may call for a data-efficient solution. A dynamic problem may call for a computationally efficient solution. And a problem that embodies the highest level of risk may call for an assured solution.

The problem and solution taxonomies incorporate both technical and informal criteria. The technical criteria are inspired by, but not directly equivalent to, such computer science concepts as *NP-hardness* (nondeterministic-polynomial-time hardness) and *Big-O complexity*. Other problem and solution characteristics are of indeterminate formality. Some problems, for instance, have rigorous formal specifications, while others are defined in part by their indeterminacy. A final

Figure 1.2
Determining Alignment Between Problem Characteristics and Solution Capabilities

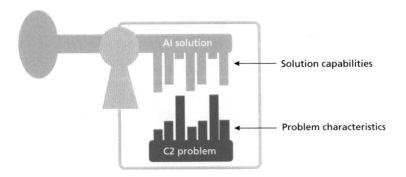

category of problem and solution characteristics resists formalization altogether. These are exemplified by those characteristics embodying qualitative value trade-offs. This is not to say that these cannot be cast into formal or quantitative terms but rather that such transmutations are inevitably artificial impositions.

Figure 1.3 displays the complete framework we propose to evaluate the efficacy of a potential solution for a particular use case. To use the framework, the analyst first works through the problem taxonomy to identify its characteristics (Step 1). Some of these problem characteristics are likely to be imperfectly known at the outset: one objective of the problem taxonomy is to illuminate these issues so that adequate attention can be directed toward them.

Once the subcategories of the problem characteristics tree have been populated, the analyst can begin considering potential solution methods (Step 2). In all but the simplest cases potential solutions will not be simple algorithms (e.g., A* search) or broad methodological

Figure 1.3
Evaluative Framework

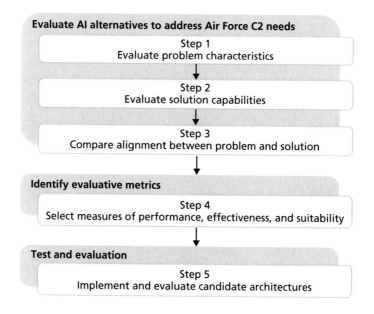

approaches (e.g., deep learning); rather, they will be architectures comprising multiple components, as well as software for implementing the algorithm and hardware on which to run the algorithm. As with problem characteristics, certain features of the solution are liable to be uncertain at first and will require additional investigation. Even so, in many cases it will immediately become apparent that a proposed solution is a poor fit for the envisioned use case. This initial weed-out process can often proceed without the need for the precise characterization of problem and solution characteristics.

Of the remaining potential solutions, further attention is given to the critical capabilities implied by the problem characteristics (Step 3). Armed with results from the first and second steps, the analyst can determine the extent to which each potential solution possesses the desired characteristics. The comparison of problem characteristics to solution capabilities ends with one of three conclusions:

- misalignment: solution X *does not apply* to problem Y
- partial alignment: solution X *conditionally applies* to problem Y if gap Z is addressed
- perfect alignment: solution X *applies* to problem Y de facto.

Ultimately one or more solution architectures are selected for full implementation—the goal of which is to enable quantitative evaluations. These evaluations must cover the AI system's performance (i.e., *Does it behave as intended?*), effectiveness (i.e., *Does it enhance the C2 process?*), and suitability (i.e., *Can it be supported and deployed?*). Identifying a sufficiently diverse set of metrics in advance of evaluation is key (Step 4). Once the solution architectures have been implemented and the evaluation metrics have been identified, the architectures can be evaluated (Step 5).

Balancing problems, solutions, and value in applied AI is not an exact science. Analysts and decisionmakers cannot escape the need to make value judgments in the face of uncertainty. The objective of our proposed framework is to make these judgments more explicit from early in the design process and to force sufficiently broad evaluations of systems once implemented.

Of note, our framework is not limited to a particular type of AI—for example, it is equally applicable to learning systems, automated planners, optimization techniques, and other computational approaches. The framework is also applicable to hybrid systems that combine multiple types of methods and algorithms and, in fact, can be used to identify components to add to a system to augment its capabilities. Finally, the framework is based on an analysis of domain-agnostic problem characteristics and solution capabilities, so it is broadly applicable.

Organization of Report

This report comprises two volumes. The first contains the primary findings and recommendations. It is designed for the policymaker. The second contains the supporting analysis. It is designed for those interested in technical details and potential extensions. The remainder of this volume follows the evaluative framework outlined in Figure 1.3:

- Chapter Two presents the taxonomy of problem characteristics and applies them to numerous games and C2 processes.
- Chapter Three presents the taxonomy of solution capabilities and applies them to numerous AI systems.
- Chapter Four presents results from an expert panel used to determine the importance of each solution capability given each problem characteristic.
- Chapter Five defines measures of performance (MoP), measures of effectiveness (MoE), and measures of suitability (MoS) used to evaluate AI systems, once implemented, and to demonstrate and socialize their utility.
- Chapter Six summarizes the work and provides recommendations.

Taxonomy of Problem Characteristics

In this chapter, we describe a taxonomy of general problem characteristics. The purpose of the taxonomy is to standardize the characterization of C2 processes in terms of the technical or mathematical challenges they entail. This is the first step toward determining which AI methods are best suited to address them.

Taxonomy and Definitions

To create a taxonomy of problem characteristics, we began by reviewing computer science, organizational science, and operations research (Table 2.1). In the early 1970s, Horst Rittle and Melvin Webber proposed ten properties to distinguish between what they referred to as "tame" and "wicked" problems.[1] Some distinguishing properties of wicked problems involve the *completeness of their specification* ("There is no definitive formulation of a wicked problem"), *goal clarity* ("Solutions to wicked problems are not true-or-false, but good-or-bad"), *relationship to past problems* ("Every wicked problem is essentially unique"), and *importance* ("The planner has no right to be wrong"). Later, in the 1990s, Stuart Russell and Peter Norvig enumerated properties of task

---

[1] H. W. J. Rittle and M. M. Webber, "Dilemmas in a General Theory of Planning," *Policy Sciences*, Vol. 4, No. 2, 1973. For a related list of properties applied to decision problems, see Y. Reich and A. Kapeliuk, "A Framework for Organizing the Space of Decision Problems with Application to Solving Subjective, Context-Dependent Problems," *Decision Support Systems*, Vol. 41, No. 1, 2005.

Table 2.1
Literature Review of Problem Characteristics

Problem Taxonomies	Description
Rittle and Webber, 1973	10 properties of planning problems that make them "wicked"
Russell and Norvig, 1995	7 properties of environments
Reich and Kapeliuk, 2005	11 characteristics of decision problems
Dulac-Arnold, Mankowitz, and Hester, 2019	9 challenges of real-world reinforcement learning

environments related to *observability* (fully versus partially observable), *action outcomes* (deterministic versus stochastic), *environment change* (static versus dynamic), and *environment complexity* (discrete versus continuous).[2]

Most recently, in 2019, Gabriel Dulac-Arnold, Daniel Mankowitz, and Todd Hester identified challenges for real-world reinforcement learning.[3] Many of the challenges they articulated overlap with those previously identified (e.g., "Reward functions are unspecified, multi-objective, or risk-sensitive"; "High-dimensional continuous state and action spaces"; "Tasks that may be partially observable, alternatively viewed as non-stationary or stochastic"; and "Safety constraints that should never or at least rarely be violated"), while others are new (e.g., "System operators who desire explainable policies and actions"). In summary, researchers have articulated a surprisingly consistent set of problem characteristics over the past 50 years and across academic fields.

Based on our review of the literature, we created a taxonomy of problem characteristics that can be grouped into four categories (Table 2.2). Some characteristics stem solely from the nature of the problem itself (e.g., operational tempo), while others incorporate value

---

[2]   Russell and Norvig, 1995.

[3]   Gabriel Dulac-Arnold, Daniel Mankowitz, and Todd Hester, *Challenges of Real-World Reinforcement Learning*, Ithaca, N.Y.: Cornell University, eprint arXiv:1904.12901, April 2019.

Table 2.2
Problem Characteristics, Descriptions, and Command and Control Examples

Grouping	Problem Characteristic	Description	C2 Example
Temporality	Operational tempo	The rate at which operations must be planned, replanned, and executed	The duration of time available for prosecuting a dynamic target
	Rate of environment change	How long it takes for the context to evolve from those previously encountered, rendering past tactics and learning outdated	How frequently rules of engagement and special operating instructions change
Complexity	Problem complexity	The combination of the size of the action space and the size of the state space	The number and types of sensors available to a commander
	Reducibility	Whether the problem can be decomposed into simpler parts	Relationships between missions and mission types that the MAAP (master air attack plan) Team must account for
Quality of information	Data availability	The quantity, quality, and representativeness of data available for training and testing	The availability of operational-level simulators suitable for training a system to perform air battle planning
	Environmental clutter/noise	Whether signals of interest are contaminated by signals from other potentially unknown and random processes	The effects of environmental noise and deliberate camouflage and concealment on intelligence assessments
	Stochasticity of action outcomes	How predictable immediate effects are based on the actions taken	Probability of kill for a kinetic or nonkinetic effect
	Clarity of goals/utility	How clearly the values of outcomes delivered during and at the end of task performance are defined	Availability of assessment data and how directly they relate to tactical tasks, operational tasks, and operational objectives
	Incompleteness of information	How much is known about the state of the environment, and about the adversary's goals and intent	The extent to which the commander lacks complete information about the battlespace or the adversary's disposition
Importance	Operational risks and benefits	The potential for the outcome to include the loss of something of value or the advantage or profit gained	The consequences of achieving or failing to achieve mission objectives

judgments (e.g., operational risks and benefits) or grant the enemy an active role (e.g., the adversary can increase environmental clutter/noise via such means as decoys and jamming). Certain characteristics tend to co-occur in problems, but all are independent of one another. Volume 2 elaborates on the definitions given in Table 2.2.

Analysis of Games and Command and Control Problems

To demonstrate the problem taxonomy, we analyzed ten games and AI test environments and ten C2 processes. The games we chose are commonly used in AI research. To rate the problem characteristics for each, we used source documents, descriptions, and experience. The C2 processes we selected span level of war (tactical, operational, and strategic) and service branches. To rate the problem characteristic for each, we used a structured protocol to interview active-duty subject-matter experts from each service. A description of these games, the formal method for scoring problem characteristics, and worked examples are provided in Volume 2.

Table 2.3 contains ratings for the ten games and C2 processes. Ratings range from 0 (*problem characteristic not present*) to 4 (*problem characteristic present to a large extent*). Strikingly, only a modest number of problem characteristics were present for each game, while most problem characteristics were present for all C2 processes. For games, 30 percent of problem characteristics received a rating greater than 0 (i.e., the characteristic was present to at least a moderate extent). The median number of characteristics present per game was 2.5 out of 10. For C2 processes, 93 percent of problem characteristics received a rating greater than 0 and the median number of characteristics present per C2 process was 9 out of 10.

Figure 2.1 shows the average ratings for problem characteristics in games and C2 processes. The average rating for operational tempo was higher for games than for C2 processes. All other problem characteristics had equal or higher ratings for C2 processes than for games.[4]

---

[4]   The variability of scores was somewhat lower for games because so many values were zero.

Table 2.3
Scoring of Problem Characteristics

Game	Operational Tempo	Rate of Environment Change	Problem Complexity	Reducibility	Data Availability	Environmental Clutter/Noise	Stochasticity of Action Outcomes	Clarity of Goals/Utility	Incompleteness of Information	Operational Risks and Benefits
Tic-tac-toe	3	0	0	0	0	0	0	0	0	0
Tetris	4	0	0	0	0	0	0	0	0	0
Checkers	3	0	2	0	0	0	0	0	0	0
Chess	3	0	2	3	0	0	0	0	0	0
Go	3	0	3	3	0	0	0	0	0	0
Texas Hold'em	3	0	2	0	0	0	2	0	3	1
CartPole-v1	4	0	3	0	0	0	0	0	0	0
HalfCheetah-v2	4	0	3	0	0	0	0	0	0	0
Bridge	3	0	2	2	2	0	2	0	4	0
StarCraft II	4	0	2	3	0	1	0	0	2	0
C2 Process										
Army Intelligence Preparation of the Battlefield	1	3	2	3	3	3	0	3	3	3
MAAP	2	2	2	2	3	1	0	1	2	3
Nuclear retargeting	3	4	2	2	3	3	1	2	3	4
Operational assessment	2	1	2	3	2	1	0	1	4	2
Personnel recovery: locate and authenticate	3	1	2	1	4	2	0	0	3	3
Reallocating ISR assets	3	2	2	3	2	2	1	1	3	2
Sensor management	3	3	2	2	2	3	1	1	2	3
Army Military Decision Making Process	1	3	2	3	3	3	1	2	2	3
Tomahawk Land Attack Missile (TLAM) planning	2	1	1	1	3	1	1	0	2	2
Troop leading procedures	2	3	1	1	4	3	1	0	2	3

Figure 2.1
Average Values of Problem Characteristics

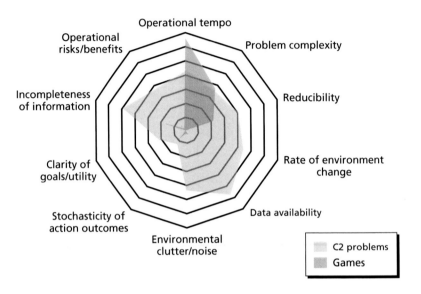

As illustrated by the figure, games of skill used to develop and demonstrate leading-edge AI systems are quantitatively and qualitatively different from C2 processes. This calls into question the generalizability of these systems to military contexts.

The ratings differed between games and C2 processes for the following reasons:

- *Operational tempo.* Most games are played in an hour or less, which places a lower limit on operational tempo. Conversely, many C2 processes take place across hours and days. Tactical processes (e.g., aircraft maneuvering) may have higher operational tempos than the C2 processes we analyzed. For example, ISR reallocation and sensor management, which are at the tactical-operational seam, did have higher operational tempos.
- *Rate of environment change.* For most games, the boards, rules, and objectives never change. Conversely, most C2 processes are affected by changes in the battle space environment and the com-

mander's guidance. For example, sensor management is affected by daily changes in enemy order of battle, rules for positive identification, and special instructions.

- *Problem complexity.* Games and C2 processes appear to have comparable levels of complexity. The environments in which C2 processes take place are far more complex than those of games, yet for operational-level planning, many low-level details of the environment can be abstracted away. For example, a TLAM navigates through a continuous state space with multiple degrees of freedom, yet the TLAM planner only has to set waypoints.
- *Reducibility.* Most games consist of one or a small number of subproblems. An exception is *StarCraft II*, which contains multiple interrelated subproblems (e.g., gathering resources, building units, and attacking). Conversely, most C2 processes include a moderate or large number of interrelated subproblems. For example, a MAAP entails planning multiple types of missions. The planning tasks are partially decomposable: each task is performed by a separate cell. Yet the cells are collocated to allow for coordination.
- *Data availability.* Because of their exact formulations, games can act as simulations for themselves. An exception is simulating human teammates in multiplayer games like bridge. Conversely, C2 processes like personnel recovery lack simulators and have only dozens of historical data points. The outputs of other processes, like the Military Decision Making Process, are neither standardized nor routinely recorded. Even for C2 problems where simulators exist (e.g., Advanced Framework for Simulation, Integration, and Modeling software for simulating aspects of sensor management, ISR reallocation, or MAAP), computational complexity can prohibit exhaustive sampling. Finally, physics-based models are more mature than adversary behavioral and statistical models.
- *Environmental clutter/noise.* Most games do not include sensory noise. Conversely, virtually all C2 processes involve environmental clutter and noise. In cases like sensor management and ISR reallocation, some sources of noise occur naturally, and others are deliberately induced by the adversary.

- *Stochasticity of action outcomes.* Some of the games we analyzed included stochastic outcomes like card draws. Of the C2 processes that we analyzed, those with actions also included a stochastic component. To deal with this stochasticity, operators are briefed on a platform's limiting factors in the case of sensor management, and they develop contingencies for launch failure in the case of TLAM planning. When commands are executed by humans, as with troop leading procedures, human behavior introduces additional uncertainty. This uncertainty is mitigated in the Military Decision Making Process by issuing execution checklists.

- *Clarity of goals/utility.* End states and objectives are clearly defined for most games. Additionally, intermediate outcomes during game play have approximate values, as captured by the blizzard score in *StarCraft II*, for example. Many C2 processes also have approximately defined utilities. For example, the Joint Integrated Prioritized Target List provides a rank-ordered list of objectives for MAAP, and track quality and coverage during sensor management can be precisely quantified. Other processes like Army Intelligence Preparation of the Battlefield have less clearly defined goals and utility.

- *Incompleteness of information.* A defining feature of some games, such as Texas Hold'em and bridge, is a high percentage of incomplete information. Nearly all C2 processes involve a moderate or high amount of incomplete information. Incompleteness arises from limited ISR coverage in operational assessment, as well as from deliberate attempts at concealment in sensor management. Incompleteness also arises from communication challenges. For example, during TLAM planning, communications are cut off when the submarine is below periscope depth.

- *Operation risks and benefits.* Games do not inherently present the potential for the loss or gain of something of value. Presumably, this is why some games have evolved to include betting. Conversely, most C2 processes present the possibility for the loss of life and equipment. These risks are greatest in the case of nuclear retargeting.

Summary

Games, problems, and C2 processes can be difficult in a variety of ways. Our analysis of ten games revealed that in most cases only one or a small number of problem characteristics were meaningfully present. Conversely, most problem characteristics were present in all C2 processes. Put simply, these C2 processes exemplify wicked problems. Complicating matters, the problem characteristics may act as amplifiers— a complex problem with high operational risks and benefits seems harder than two separate problems, one that is complex and the other with high operational risks and benefits.

The results from our analysis do not detract from the significance of highly capable AI in games. Yet they clearly illustrate the leap needed to apply AI to C2. As an interim step, the Air Force could focus on C2 processes that present a more limited number of problem characteristics. Alternatively, the Air Force could develop human-machine teaming constructs in which AI is only applied to suitable subtasks within larger C2 processes.

Taxonomy of Solution Capabilities

In this chapter, we describe a taxonomy of solution capabilities. The purpose of the taxonomy is to standardize the characterization of computational architectures, whether they use one or multiple algorithmic approaches, in terms of the capabilities they afford. This is the second step toward determining whether an AI system that is potentially suitable for a C2 process can in fact be implemented.

Taxonomy and Definitions

To create a taxonomy of solution capabilities, we began by reviewing computer science and cognitive science literature (Table 3.1). Russell and Norvig provide the seminal index of AI capabilities, broken out by functional category.[1] Some of these categories involve perceiving, reasoning, planning, and acting, and they are strikingly similar to those identified in texts on the human cognitive architecture (although the functions are accomplished differently in situ versus in silico).[2] A similar functional decomposition is evident in the Defense Science Board's four-category characterization of autonomous system technologies into sense, think/decide, act, and team.[3]

---

[1] Russell and Norvig, 1995.

[2] J. R. Anderson, *Cognitive Psychology and Its Implications*, New York: Macmillan, 2005.

[3] Defense Science Board, 2016.

Table 3.1
Literature Review of Solution Capabilities

Problem Taxonomies	Description
Russell and Norvig, 1995	Problem-solving, reasoning, planning, learning, communicating, perceiving, acting
Anderson, 2005	Perception, memory, problem-solving, reasoning and decisionmaking, language, movement
Dahm, 2010	Trusted, adaptive, and flexible
Defense Science Board, 2016	Sense, think/decide, act, team
McKinsey Global Institute et al., 2017	Machine learning, computer vision, natural language, smart robotics, autonomous vehicles, virtual agents
Zacharias, 2019a	Properties for proficiency, tenets of trust, principles of flexibility

In *Autonomous Horizons: The Way Forward*, Greg L. Zacharias, the chief scientist of the U.S. Air Force, presented a different set of requirements for autonomous systems grouped among properties for proficiency, tenets of trust, and principles of flexibility.[4] These are consistent with the call in *Technology Horizons* for trusted, adaptive, and flexible autonomous systems.[5] The requirements identified by the U.S. Air Force chief scientist are consistent with functional capabilities—which contribute to an autonomous system's proficiency, flexibility, and trustworthiness—identified in the computer science and cognitive science literature.

Finally, in a 2016 review of commercial investments in AI-focused companies, the McKinsey Global Institute presented yet another grouping of solution capabilities by business use case.[6]

Based on our review of the literature, we created a taxonomy of solution capabilities that can be grouped into four categories (Table 3.2).

---

[4] Zacharias, 2019a.

[5] Dahm, 2010.

[6] McKinsey Global Institute, Jacques Bughin, Eric Hazan, Sree Ramaswamy, Michael Chui, Tera Allas, Peter Dahlström, Nicolaus Henke, and Monica Trench, *Artificial Intelligence: The Next Digital Frontier?*, New York: McKinsey & Company, June 2017.

Table 3.2
Solution Capabilities and Definitions

Grouping	Problem Characteristic	Description	C2 Example
Complexity	Computational efficiency	How the amount of time/memory that a system needs scales with the size of the problem	The time for a computational air battle planner to return a complete MAAP
Performance	Data efficiency	The amount of training data that a system needs to produce acceptable-quality solutions	The number of labeled samples needed to train a deep neural network to classify adversary equipment
	Soundness	The quality of a system with inference rules that return only valid solutions	Whether a computational air battle planner returns MAAPs that can be executed given special operating instructions, friendly order of battle, and other constraints
	Optimality	The quality of a system with inference rules that produce the maximum value for the objective function	Whether a computational air battle planner returns a MAAP that maximizes the total value of all completed missions
Flexibility	Robustness	The ability to produce reasonable outputs and/or degrade gracefully under unanticipated circumstances	How the performance of a trained classifier changes when environmental conditions in imagery vary
	Learning	The ability to improve performance through training and/or experience	Whether a computational air battle manager can learn to improve its performance in simulation and/or in situ
Practicality	Explainability	The ability of an expert human to understand why the system produces the outputs it does	Whether a human analyst can understand why a computational air battle planner recommended aspects of the plan that it did
	Assuredness	The ability of an expert human to determine that the system operates as intended	Whether a computational air battle manager can be verified and validated during test and evaluation and whether those assurances can be maintained once it has been deployed.

The purpose of the taxonomy is to determine whether a potential solution addresses the problem characteristics defined in the previous chapter. Volume 2 elaborates on the definitions given in Table 3.2.

Analysis of Artificial Intelligence Systems

To demonstrate the solution taxonomy, we analyzed ten AI systems. The systems we chose vary in their use of classic versus contemporary AI techniques, their reliance on knowledge engineering versus learning, and their suitability for reactive, planning, and classification-type tasks. To rate the solution capabilities for each system, we used source code, published descriptions, and a structured protocol to interview an AI researcher from RAND knowledgeable about the system. A description of these systems, the formal method for scoring solution capabilities, and worked examples are provided in Volume 2.

Table 3.3 contains ratings for the ten AI systems. Ratings range from 0 (*solution capability not present*) to 4 (*solution capability pres-*

Table 3.3
Scoring of Solution Capabilities

AI System	Computational Efficiency	Soundness	Optimality	Data Efficiency	Robustness	Learning	Explainability	Assuredness
Deep Q-Learning	4	1	3	0	0	3	0	0
AlphaZero	3	4	3	0	0	3	0	0
Instance-based learning	2	1	1	2	2	3	2	0
Recurrent neural network	4	1	3	1	1	3	0	0
Iterated-Width Planning	1	4	3	4	3	0	3	3
Alpha-beta pruning	3	4	2	4	2	0	4	4
Mixed integer program (MIP)	0	4	4	4	2	0	3	4
Greedy heuristic	4	4	1	4	2	0	4	4
Influence network	1	4	4	3	2	0	3	4
Genetic algorithm	2	3	2	3	1	0	0	1

ent to a large extent). The mean rating across systems and capabilities equaled 2.1 out of 4, and no single system had all capabilities. The ratings illustrate a general trade-off between systems that learn and systems that do not. As compared with systems that learn, systems that do not have higher average ratings for data efficiency (3.7 versus 0.8), assuredness (3.3 versus 0), soundness (3.8 versus 1.8), and explainability (2.8 versus −0.8). Conversely, systems that do not learn have lower average ratings for computational efficiency (1.8 versus 3.3) and similar average ratings for optimality (2.7 versus 2.5) and robustness (2 versus 0.8).

Figure 3.1 shows the average ratings for solution capabilities across all AI systems. Overall, the systems had highest average ratings for soundness, optimality, and data efficiency. The finding that data efficiency was rated relatively high and learning was rated relatively low reflects the different numbers of learning and nonlearning systems included in the sample (four and six, respectively). Robustness had moderate-to-low ratings for learning and nonlearning systems alike.

Figure 3.1
Average Values of Solution Capabilities

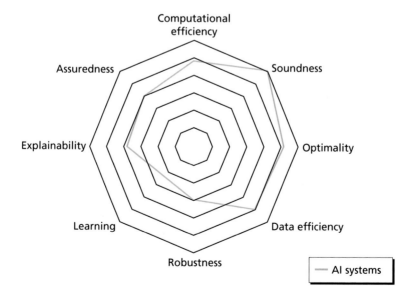

Summary

Computer science research has primarily focused on the ability of an AI system to optimize some objective function. However, other important solution capabilities exist. Based on our evaluation of AI systems, no one system typically has all capabilities. And so the choice of a system embodies a decision about which capabilities to trade off. The most striking trade-off in the sample of ten systems that we analyzed was between learning on the one hand and data efficiency, sound, assured, and explainability on the other hand. The implication here is twofold: systems for real-world AI must be evaluated along multiple dimensions, and the system with the highest level of performance may not be the preferred solution.

CHAPTER FOUR

Mapping Problem Characteristics to Solution Capabilities

The previous chapters present two complementary taxonomies for problem characteristics and solution capabilities. We hypothesized that different problem characteristics call for different solution capabilities. As a key fits a lock, the capabilities of an AI system must be aligned with the characteristics of a C2 problem. The existing literature does not provide such a crosswalk. In this chapter, we report results from an expert panel conducted to determine which solution capabilities are most important for each problem characteristic. Based on the results of the panel, we present a method for scoring the suitability of an AI system for a particular C2 problem.

Expert Panel on Artificial Intelligence for Command and Control

Expert Sample and Panel Design

We invited 50 individuals from Federally Funded Research and Development Centers, government laboratories, academia, industry, and military services to participate in an expert panel on AI for C2. All participants were experienced AI researchers. These experts came from diverse backgrounds: 20 were from Federally Funded Research and Development Centers, 6 were from active-duty military service, 5 were from industry, 12 were from government laboratories, and 6 were from academia. About two-thirds were knowledgeable about C2 processes, but given the general nature of the problem characteristics and solution capabilities, C2 expertise was not needed to participate.

The panel featured an embedded mixed-methods design and followed established practices for eliciting expert judgments.[1] Quantitative data were used to determine the importance of solution capabilities for each problem characteristic, and qualitative data were used to understand factors influencing those ratings. Experts completed two rating rounds interspersed with a discussion round (Figure 4.1).

In the first round, experts reviewed definitions of all problem characteristics and solution capabilities. The instructions explained that the purpose of the panel was to determine the importance of each solution capability for each problem characteristic. Experts were presented with all 80 pair-wise combinations of problem characteristics and solution capabilities, and they rated and commented on the importance of the solution capability for each pair. Experts used nine-point scales to rate the importance of the solution capability given the problem characteristic. The scale ranged from *not important* (ratings 1 to 3),

Figure 4.1
Expert Panel Protocol

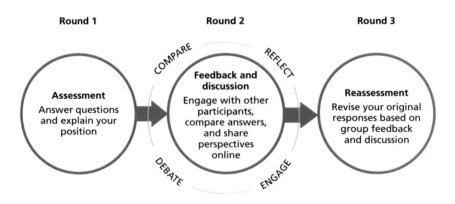

[1] Kathryn Fitch, Steven J. Bernstein, Maria Dolores Aguilar, Bernard Burnand, Juan Ramon LaCalle, Pablo Lazaro, Mirjam van het Loo, Joseph McDonnell, Janneke Vader, and James P. Kahan, *The RAND/UCLA Appropriateness Method User's Manual*, Santa Monica, Calif.: RAND Corporation, MR-1269-DG-XII/RE, 2001.

to *moderately important* (ratings 4 to 6), to *extremely important* (ratings 7 to 9). Experts were asked to explain their ratings and list the factors that most strongly influenced their responses.

In the second round, experts reviewed bar charts showing their own responses along with others' responses. We thematically analyzed comments from this round and displayed summaries beside the corresponding bar charts. Summaries showed the most common thematic responses by quantile (i.e., low, medium, or high importance). Finally, experts discussed the results of this round using asynchronous and moderated discussion boards. In the third round, experts were allowed to revise their original ratings based on feedback and discussion from the second round. Once again, experts were asked to explain their ratings.

To assess the importance of solution capabilities for each problem characteristic, we adopted the analytical approach used previously in expert panel studies.[2] Additional details about the panel design, online platform, and data analysis approach are reported in Volume 2.

Data Analysis and Results

Figure 4.2 shows median ratings for all problem-solution pairs after the final round. Red and yellow indicate high and low importance, respectively. Bolded cells correspond to the 36 pairs where the solution capability was rated as extremely important for the corresponding problem characteristic. Two problem characteristics, *complex* and *high risks/benefits*, were especially demanding in terms of the number of solution capabilities they called for (6 and 5, respectively). Additionally, two solutions capabilities, *robust* and *assured*, were especially pervasive in terms of the number of problem characteristics they were essential to (9 and 7, respectively). These results have two implications: First, problems that are complex and that have high risks/benefits may present the greatest challenges for AI systems. Second, investments to increase the robustness and assuredness of AI systems will be broadly

---

[2] D. Khodyakov, S. Grant, B. Denger, K. Kinnett, A. Martin, M. Booth, C. Armstrong, E. Dao, C. Chen, I. Coulter, H. Peay, G. Hazlewood, and N. Street, "Using an Online, Modified Delphi Approach to Engage Patients and Caregivers in Determining the Patient-Centeredness of Duchenne Muscular Dystrophy Care Considerations," *Medical Decision Making*, Vol. 39, No. 8, 2019.

Figure 4.2
Median Ratings of Importance by Problem-Solution Pair

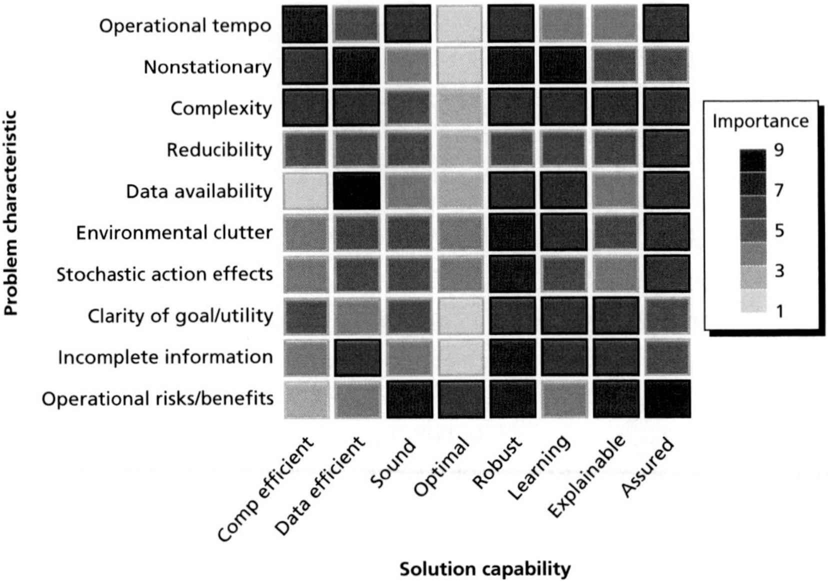

beneficial. More detail about expert ratings and free responses may be found in Volume 2.

Scoring Alignment Between Command and Control Processes and Artificial Intelligence Systems

The results from the expert panel enable a general and systematic way to judge the suitability of an AI system for a given problem. We demonstrate the method with three worked examples, beginning with AI for computer chess and ending with AI for C2. The first example involves applying alpha-beta pruning to the game of chess. The method is as follows:

- *Rate the problem characteristics.* Volume 2 lists ratings for the ten problem characteristics for chess. We duplicate these values down the column labeled "Rating" in Table 4.1.

Table 4.1
Determining the Suitability of Alpha-Beta Pruning for Chess

Problem Characteristic	Solution Capability	Computational Efficiency	Data Efficiency	Soundness	Optimality	Robustness	Learning	Explainability	Assuredness	
	Rating	3	4	4	2	2	0	4	4	
Operational tempo	3	9		12		6			12	
Rate of environment change	0	0	0			0	0			
Problem complexity	2	6	8			4	0	8	8	
Reducibility	3								12	
Data availability	0		0			0	0		0	
Environmental clutter/noise	0					0	0		0	
Stochasticity of action outcomes	0					0			0	
Clarity of goals and utility	0					0	0	0		
Incompleteness of information	0		0			0	0	0		
Operational risks and benefits	0			0	0	0		0	0	
Alpha-beta pruning total	15	8	12	0	10	0	8	32	85	

- *Rate the solution capabilities.* Volume 2 lists ratings for the eight solution capabilities for alpha-beta pruning. We duplicate these values across the row labeled "Rating" in Table 4.1.
- *Multiply the values of problem characteristics by the values of solution capabilities.* We then multiply ratings for problem characteristics in chess with ratings for solution capabilities in alpha-beta pruning. Note that we only do this for the 36 critical problem-solution pairs identified by the expert panel, which are shaded in gray in Table 4.1.
- *Sum over the critical pairs.* The bottom row of Table 4.1 provides the sum of scores for each column. The right-most value in the bottom row is the sum across all columns and represents a composite measure of alpha-beta pruning's suitability for chess.

In this example, the suitability score of alpha-beta pruning for chess equals 85. Three problem characteristics are present in chess (i.e., operational tempo, problem complexity, and reducibility). Based on the critical pairs, these characteristics call for all solution capabilities except for optimality. Alpha-beta pruning has most of these capabilities and so is suitable for chess.

For comparison, Table 4.2 shows the suitability of AlphaZero for chess. Surprisingly, its suitability score is far lower. AlphaZero is a stronger chess player than alpha-beta pruning—this is reflected in its greater optimality rating. Yet the one problem characteristic that calls for optimal solutions—operational risks and benefits—is not present in chess. Conversely, alpha-beta pruning is more explainable and assured than AlphaZero. Because these solution capabilities *are* called for by characteristics present in chess, alpha-beta pruning receives a higher suitability score.

One could argue that research on computer chess artificially elevates operational risks and benefits to the highest level—maximum performance is effectively (if not logically) paramount. If the value assigned to operational risks and benefits is increased to 4, the new suitability scores for alpha-beta pruning and AlphaZero change to 149 and 61, respectively. In other words, the gap between alpha-beta pruning and AlphaZero *increases*. Among other things, operational risks and benefits call for solutions that are (i) optimal, (ii) explainable, and (iii) assured. AlphaZero has an advantage relative to alpha-beta pruning in terms of optimality, whereas alpha-beta pruning has relative advantages in terms of explainability and assuredness.[3] The somewhat counterintuitive finding that alpha-beta pruning has a higher suitability score reflects the fact that the superiority of AlphaZero has been demonstrated in the rarefied context of game play, whereas our method is intended to evaluate real-world AI.

---

[3] One could argue that the assessment of optimality for alpha-beta pruning was too generous and the assessment for AlphaZero was too harsh. If we set the values of optimality to 1 and 4, respectively, the new suitability scores still strongly favor alpha-beta pruning (145 versus 65).

Table 4.2
Determining the Suitability of AlphaZero for Chess

Problem Characteristic	Solution Capability / Rating	Computational Efficiency	Data Efficiency	Soundness	Optimality	Robustness	Learning	Explainability	Assuredness	
	Rating	3	0	4	3	0	3	0	0	
Operational tempo	3	9		12		0			0	
Rate of environment change	0	0	0			0	0			
Problem complexity	2	6	0			0	6	0	0	
Reducibility	3								0	
Data availability	0		0			0	0		0	
Environmental clutter/noise	0					0	0		0	
Stochasticity of action outcomes	0					0			0	
Clarity of goals and utility	0					0	0	0		
Incompleteness of information	0		0			0	0	0		
Operational risks and benefits	0			0	0	0		0	0	
AlphaZero total		15	0	12	0	0	6	0	0	33

This method can be used to determine the suitability of AI systems for C2 processes as well. Table 4.3 compares two computational solutions, a MIP and a greedy heuristic, for MAAP.[4] As shown in the second column of the table, most problem characteristics are present to a moderate or high extent for MAAP. Accordingly, every problem characteristic is called for. As shown in the second row of the table, solution capabilities differ between the MIP and the heuristic.

Overall, the suitability score of the MIP for MAAP is lower than that for the heuristic. The difference can be understood in terms of

---

[4]   Additional details about the MIP and the heuristic are provided in Volume 2.

Table 4.3
Determining the Suitability of a Mixed-Integer Program and a Greedy Heuristic for a Master Air Attack Plan

Problem Characteristic	Solution Capability	Computational Efficiency	Data Efficiency	Soundness	Optimality	Robustness	Learning	Explainability	Assuredness	
	Rating	0, 4	4, 4	4, 4	4, 1	2, 2	0, 0	3, 4	4, 4	
Operational tempo	2	0, 8		8, 8		4, 4			8, 8	
Rate of environment change	2	0, 8	8, 8			4, 4	0, 0			
Problem complexity	2	0, 8	8, 8			4, 4	0, 0	6, 8	8, 8	
Reducibility	2								8, 8	
Data availability	3		12, 12			6, 6	0, 0		12, 12	
Environmental clutter/noise	1					2, 2	0, 0		4, 4	
Stochasticity of action outcomes	0					0, 0			0, 0	
Clarity of goals and utility	1					2, 2	0, 0	3, 4		
Incompleteness of information	2		8, 8			4, 4	0, 0	6, 8		
Operational risks and benefits	3			12, 12	12, 3	6, 6		9, 12	12, 12	
MIP total		0	36	20	12	32	0	24	52	176
Heuristic total	24	36	20	3	32	0	32	52	199	

NOTE: The first value in each cell is for the MIP, and the second value in each cell is for the heuristic.

the system's different capabilities. The MIP was rated higher for optimality, whereas the heuristic was rated higher for computational efficiency and explainability. Given the problem characteristics embodied in MAAP, the latter two capabilities, computational efficiency and explainability, are more important than optimality.

Finally, this method can be used to determine which solution capabilities are most called for across a collection of problems or processes. Chapter Two contains an analysis of problem characteristics for ten games and C2 processes (Table 2.3). The results from that analysis combined with the 36 critical problem-solution pairs identified by the expert panel can be used to determine the relative importance of the eight solution capabilities for each set of problems.

Figure 4.3 shows the importance of the eight solution capabilities separately for games and C2 processes.[5] Values are higher for C2 processes—because they embody more problem characteristics, they also call for more solution capabilities. Games of strategy and

Figure 4.3
Relative Importance of Solution Capabilities Across Ten Command and Control Processes and Games, and Capabilities of Artificial Intelligence Systems Analyzed

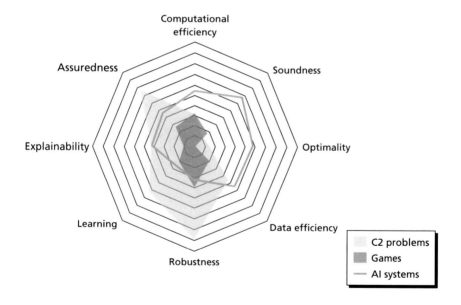

---

[5] For each solution capability, we determined the problem characteristics that called for it. We then summed across the ratings for those problem characteristics for a given game or C2 process. For example, computational efficiency is called for by problems with high operational tempo, high rate of environment change, and high complexity. The importance of computational efficiency for MAAP equals 2 + 2 + 2, or 6 (Table 4.3). The values shown in Figure 4.3 reflect the average importance of each capability taken across the ten games and the ten C2 processes.

C2 problems both call for basic capabilities like computational efficiency, soundness, and optimality. However, C2 processes call for additional advanced capabilities like robustness, assuredness, learning, and explainability.

Figure 4.3 also shows capabilities averaged across the ten AI systems described earlier (Table 3.3). The AI systems place relatively greater emphasis on soundness and optimality than the C2 processes call for, while they place relatively less emphasis on robustness, assuredness, and learning. Collectively, these results suggest that certain AI systems optimized for game play, in their current form, may be of limited use to DoD.

Summary

Problems can be difficult in a variety of ways, and different AI systems have different capabilities. The suitability of an AI system for a given problem depends on the alignment between its capabilities and the problem's characteristics. All solution capabilities are desirable, but the ones that are essential depend on characteristics of a particular problem. For example, a problem with low data availability calls for a system that is data efficient, a problem with high operational tempo calls for a system that is computationally efficient, and a problem with high operational risks and benefits calls for a system that is sound. These solution capabilities—data efficiency, computational efficiency, and soundness—seem less critical for a problem with abundant historical data, ample time to respond, and little consequence.

Though useful in its own right, the method is limited in certain ways that remain to be addressed in future research:

- *Qualitative nature of problem and solution ratings.* Presently, the ratings assigned to problem characteristics and solution capabilities are based on expert judgment. A corresponding set of quantitative metrics could be derived for the dimensions.
- *Weighting function.* Presently, we applied a threshold to define critical pairings of problem characteristics and solution capabilities,

and we assigned uniform weight to those pairs. Alternate weighting functions that give continuously varying values to different pairs could be used as well.

- *Contextual variation in problem characteristics.* The results of the analysis depend on assumptions about problem characteristics, which are assumed to be constant. If the characteristics of a C2 problem vary by context—as might be the case, for instance, if a commander has initiative versus if they are trying to seize it— then the results of the analysis will vary by context as well.

Notwithstanding these limitations, the method provides a systematic way to relate problem characteristics to AI capabilities and to trace results back to assumptions about each.

Metrics for Evaluating Artificial Intelligence Solutions

In the preceding chapters, we showed that different combinations of C2 problem characteristics call for different combinations of AI solution capabilities, and we described a method for selecting an AI solution that is likely to fit the C2 problem. In this chapter, we look more closely at certain aspects of this fit and propose three categories of assessment measures for AI solutions to help complete the selection process. Establishing assessment measures *in advance* helps to ensure that development progress is evaluated fairly and that potential implementation issues are identified. We discuss each category in detail and highlight specific metrics that are of particular importance to AI solutions.

From our review of the strategic guidance on AI solutions, our review of documents on C2 problems, and discussions with subject-matter experts (see Volume 2), we find that three broad categories of measure are needed to assess the utility of AI-enabled C2 systems in operational contexts: MoE, MoP, and MoS. All three categories of measures are important to properly evaluate progress and identify shortfalls. For our purposes, we define these categories in accordance with the Defense Acquisition University glossary, as shown in Table 5.1.[1]

---

[1] DoD, *Glossary of Defense Acquisition Acronyms and Terms*, Fort Belvoir, Va.: Defense Acquisition University, 2017b.

Table 5.1
Categories of Measure

Category	Definition
MoE	The data used to measure the military effect (mission accomplishment) that comes from the use of the system in its expected environment. That environment includes the system under test and all interrelated systems, that is, the planned or expected environment in terms of weapons, sensors, C2, and platforms, as appropriate, needed to accomplish an end-to-end mission in combat.
MoP	System-particular performance parameters, such as speed, payload, range, time on station, frequency, or other distinctly quantifiable performance features.
MoS	Measure of an item's ability to be supported in its intended operational environment. MoS typically relate to readiness or operational availability and, hence, reliability, maintainability, and the item's support structure.

SOURCE: DoD, 2017.

Measures of Effectiveness

MoE capture the underlying reasons why change is needed—to use a market analogy, they represent the "demand" signal. In the context of C2 systems, these are measures of how well the system supports what is otherwise operationally executable. MoE are typically familiar measures of mission success derived from the C2 problem itself, such as survivability and force exchange ratios. MoE should be independent of the proposed solution: they should apply equally well to any proposed doctrine, organization, training, materiel, leadership and education, personnel, facilities, and policy solution. MoE can also be used to benchmark the performance of the current C2 system.[2]

Careful consideration of MoE is important to ensure that the proposed AI solution addresses the right C2 problem. Quantifying and standardizing MoE is challenging, however. From our review of the C2 literature, we identified two main challenges to doing so:

---

[2] MoE cannot be derived from the C2 problem characteristics discussed in Chapter Two. Those characteristics describe the mathematical nature of the problem, but they do not capture the associated military benefits—for example, improved outcomes.

(1) the inherent complexity of C2 systems and (2) the wide variety of C2 missions.

The largest challenge in measuring C2 systems is the inherent complexity of those systems.[3] C2 systems involve many coordinated processes, require human decisionmaking, and are subject to such external factors as environmental conditions and adversary actions. To isolate the effect of a single change to the C2 system while controlling for all other variables is often not feasible. As the North Atlantic Treaty Organization code of best practices for C2 assessment explains,

> C2 issues differ in fundamental ways from physics dominated problems. C2 deals with distributed teams of humans operating under stress and in a variety of other operating conditions. C2 problems are thus dominated by their information, behavioural, and cognitive aspects that have been less well researched and understood. This focus creates a multidimensional, complex analytic space.[4]

The second major challenge is that different missions call for different metrics. For example, traditional C2 metrics, such as mission success and force exchange ratios, are not relevant for humanitarian assistance/disaster relief operations, which may themselves require a different set of metrics than peacekeeping operations. Furthermore, changes to C2 processes may alter effectiveness differently in different missions.

For these reasons, no single, standard set of MoE can be derived for *all* C2 problems: MoE must be tailored for each mission. In light of this, we do not provide a fixed list of MoE but rather a set of subcategories and questions that should be considered when devising them. Our goal here is to identify groups broad enough to be applicable to most C2 functions and to cover the areas in which we anticipate AI solutions

---

[3] A C2 system "consists of the facilities; equipment; communications; staff functions and procedures; and personnel essential for planning, preparing for, monitoring, and assessing operations." Joint Publication 3-0, 2017.

[4] North Atlantic Treaty Organization, *Code of Best Practice for C2 Assessment*, Brussels: Research and Technology Organization, 2002.

Table 5.2
Measures of Effectiveness

Group	Assessment Question	Examples of Metrics
Decision quality	*Does the C2 system make the best decision possible given the information available?*	• Closeness to optimal decision, outcome • Robustness of decision against range of operational considerations • Number of courses of action considered • Comparisons with historical benchmarks or other decisionmaking processes
Situational awareness	*Is the information available to the C2 system accurate, complete, and current?*	• Probability of detection • False alarm rate • Currency of common operational picture • Various ISR and data quality metrics
Timeliness	*How quickly does the C2 system process the information available to make decisions?*	• Speed of C2 process • Relative speed of the observe, orient, decide, and act (OODA) loop compared with that of the adversary
Survivability/ lethality	*How does the C2 system contribute to the survivability and lethality of the force?*	• Probability of survival • Force-loss exchange ratios • Various battle damage assessment metrics
Resource management	*How well does the C2 system use available resources?*	• Efficiency of resource allocation • Number of different missions pursued or not pursued due to resource availability • Opportunity costs

will be most appropriate. These different groups are listed in Table 5.2, and we discuss each in more detail below.

Decision quality is perhaps the most direct measure of an effective C2 process. U.S. Marine Corps doctrine holds that "a principal aim of command and control is to enhance the commander's ability to make sound and timely decisions,"[5] while joint doctrine notes that "the C2 function supports an efficient decision-making process."[6] The relevant question here is whether the choice made was the best one possible given the information available. However, determining whether this

---

[5]   U.S. Marine Corps, *Command and Control*, Doctrinal Publication 6, Washington, D.C., 2018.

[6]   Joint Publication 3-0, 2017.

is so—or quantifying how far from optimal a decision may be—is difficult.

Mission outcomes are often used as a way to evaluate decision quality. While mission outcomes can provide an indication of good decision-making, they also can be misleading. Missions may succeed or fail due to external factors that are unknown or unknowable at the time that decisions must be made: changing environmental conditions and adversary actions can conceal the effects of both good decisions and bad ones. (As the saying goes, the enemy gets a vote.) For these reasons, experts caution against using outcomes as the only measure of C2 effectiveness: "While mission outcomes should be a factor in the equation, the quality of C2 should not be deduced solely from mission outcomes."[7]

But there are other ways to assess decision quality. Modeling and simulation can be used to assess whether a decision would have been good under other conditions—that is, to determine its robustness—and to evaluate the effects of actions *not* taken.[8] Comparisons with historical examples or other decisionmaking processes can also be helpful. However, none of these methods are generalizable or prescriptive: they must be tailored to a particular situation.

Situational awareness is also an essential part of an effective C2 process. While decision quality concerns the optimality of the decision made given the information available, situational awareness concerns underlying information flow. As Air Force doctrine states: "Fluid horizontal and vertical information flow enables effective C2 throughout the chain of command. This information flow, and its timely fusion, enables optimum decision-making."[9]

---

[7]   David S. Alberts and Richard E. Hayes, *Understanding Command and Control*, Washington, D.C.: Command and Control Research Program, 2006.

[8]   Abbie Tingstad, Dahlia Anne Goldfeld, Lance Menthe, Robert A. Guffey, Zachary Haldeman, Krista S. Langeland, Amado Cordova, Elizabeth M. Waina, and Balys Gintautas, *Assessing the Value of Intelligence Collected by U.S. Air Force Airborne Intelligence, Surveillance, and Reconnaissance Platforms*, Santa Monica, Calif.: RAND Corporation, RR-2742-AF, 2021.

[9]   U.S. Air Force Doctrine, *Annex 3-30: Command and Control*, Maxwell Air Force Base, Ala.: Lemay Center for Doctrine, 2020.

Situational awareness is commonly defined as "the perception of the elements in the environment within a volume of time and space, the comprehension of their meaning, and the projection of their status in the near future."[10] Although *situational awareness* is often synonymous with the *commander's knowledge*, situational awareness includes other processes associated with collecting and understanding information, for example, a collection management strategy that resolves priority information requests. For this reason, proxy metrics for situational awareness often include the dimensions of data quality: accuracy, completeness, consistency, timeliness, uniqueness, and validity.[11] It is important to note, however, that not all C2 processes affect situational awareness, so this group is not always needed to assess a specific C2 problem.

Timeliness refers to the speed with which the C2 system completes, or contributes to the completion of, the entire OODA loop.[12] According to Army doctrine, "Timely decisions and actions are essential for effective command and control."[13] While timeliness is a part of situational awareness, this group focuses on the speed of the C2 process. Timeliness is about getting the right information to the right people, so they can make the necessary decisions *before it is too late*—in other words, timeliness is about getting inside the adversary's OODA loop. Or, as Marine doctrine puts it,

> Whatever the age or technology, effective command and control will come down to people using information to decide and act wisely. And whatever the age or technology, the ultimate measure

---

[10] Mica R. Endsley, "Design and Evaluation for Situation Awareness Enhancement," *Proceedings of the Human Factors Society Annual Meeting*, Vol. 32, No. 2, 1988.

[11] There are many definitions of the dimensions of data quality. An often-cited paper is Nicola Askham, Denise Cook, Martin Doyle, Helen Fereday, Mike Gibson, Ulrich Landbeck, Rob Lee, Chris Maynard, Gary Palmer, and Julian Schwarzenbach, *The Six Primary Dimensions for Data Quality Assessment: Data Quality Dimensions*, Bristol, U.K.: Data Management Association and Data Quality Dimensions Working Group, October 2013.

[12] John R. Boyd, "Patterns of Conflict," unpublished briefing slides, 1986.

[13] Army Doctrine Publication 6-0, *Mission Command: Command and Control of Army Forces*, Washington, D.C.: U.S. Department of the Army, 2019.

of command and control effectiveness will always be the same: Can it help us act faster and more effectively than the enemy?[14]

Survivability/lethality is a measure that applies to most force-on-force missions and to some noncombat missions as well. There may be a trade-off between survivability and other measures of effectiveness:

> Command post survivability is vital to mission success and is measured by the capabilities of the threat in the context of the situation. Survivability may be obtained at the price of effectiveness.[15]

However, as with situational awareness, it should be noted that not all C2 processes affect the survivability of the force, particularly in military operations other than war. Furthermore, it is important to note that many traditional measures, such as force exchange ratio, are no longer considered adequate to the growing complexity of warfare.[16] For this reason, this group is not always relevant to a specific C2 problem.

Finally, C2 relies on effective *resource management* in many areas. There are often important trade-offs in how resources are allocated: focusing on achieving one objective may limit the ability to achieve another objective. As David Alberts and Richard Hayes explained,

> There are many ways to allocate resources among entities and there are many ways resources are matched to tasks. Each of these has the potential to result in different degrees of effectiveness and/or agility. . . . How well resources are allocated and utilized is often the determining factor in whether or not the intended purpose is achieved.[17]

---

[14] U.S. Marine Corps, 2018.

[15] Army Doctrine Publication 6-0, 2019.

[16] Alberts and Hayes, 2006.

[17] Alberts and Hayes, 2006, pp. 46–47.

Here we refer to how efficiently resources are employed and what trade-offs must be made to obtain them, including opportunity costs. These measures are of particular importance for C2 of logistics processes.

Measures of Performance

MoP capture the power of the proposed AI solution—to use a market analogy, they represent the "supply" that is offered. Typically, MoP are familiar measures of software and hardware, focusing, for instance, on such issues as run time and error rates. Because MoP align well with software development, they are often used to define requirements for the acquisition process. However, since the ultimate goal is to satisfy the MoE, MoP are better understood as proxy metrics: the bars should be set high enough to ensure high confidence that the MoE will be satisfied.

In our review of AI proposals described later in this chapter, we found that most AI metrics in use today—and especially for ML—revolve around solution accuracy. But, as Kri Wagstaff points out, "Suites of experiments are often summarized by the average accuracy across all data sets. This tells us nothing at all useful about generalization or impact, since the meaning of an X% improvement may be very different for different data sets."[18] Table 5.3 summarizes the different types of MoP we identified from the AI solution capabilities.[19]

The MoP derive directly from the AI solution capabilities that we discussed in detail in Chapter Three and are defined in more rigorous quantitative terms. Two additional points are worth noting.

First, as mentioned above, accuracy is the most common type of AI measure. In our scheme, accuracy derives from two AI capabilities—soundness and optimality—but the distinction is not essential. What matters more is that choosing which accuracy metrics to use requires

---

[18] Kri L. Wagstaff, "Machine Learning that Matters," *Proceedings of the 29th International Conference on Machine Learning*, Madison, Wisc.: Omnipress, 2012.

[19] Note that categories associated with practicality—V&V and explainability—are missing from this list because they are not truly benchmarks or properties of the algorithm itself. V&V is an activity performed on the algorithm, and explainability is about human understanding of the process. We include these as MoS (see next section).

Table 5.3
Measures of Performance

AI Solution Capability	Examples of Metrics
Computational efficiency	• Run time • Speed of computation as a function of input • System requirements (memory, processors, storage)
Data efficiency	• Labeled training data required per object class
Soundness	• Completeness (e.g., number of feasible alternatives found) • Error rate
Optimality	• Probability of detection • Geolocation accuracy
Robustness	• How other MoP vary when the algorithm is run against *new* data sets
Learning	• How other MoP vary when additional examples are provided to the algorithm from the *original* data set on which it was trained

a clear understanding of the goal of the algorithm and the costs of an incorrect output. Some applications may require a low false positive rate, while others may require a low false negative rate. These requirements must be known and understood when developing metrics and criteria.

Second, algorithm performance will rely heavily on the data that are input into the model. If these data are not understood by the developers or the users, they could lead to poor results. For example, a largely unbalanced data set may require additional methods to better train the model.[20] The accurate assessment of MoP requires a high-quality data set. Accordingly, data sets should be examined to ensure that they are characterized by minimal bias, balance, relevancy, sufficiency, and so on.

Measures of Suitability

MoS capture the range of operational conditions under which an AI solution must be able to solve a C2 problem. Typically, MoS are famil-

---

[20] An unbalanced data set is one in with an unequal distribution of classes—for example, few instances of radar sites in an image classification library.

iar measures of system integration, such as interoperability and all the other "-ilities":[21] as one study described it, "Algorithms should undergo the '-ilities' test. The test looks at reliability, accountability, maintainability, functionality." For these standard categories of operational conditions, which can and should apply to almost any acquisition program, we reviewed DoD acquisition literature, most notably Defense Acquisition University guidance.

For AI systems, however, certain other operational conditions are of particular importance as well. We identified those conditions during our review of the AI strategy documents, as described above. Table 5.4 shows all MoS groups. We have grouped some of the -ilities together: because these definitions were originally designed for hardware, they are less distinct for software-based systems—so often one subgroup will suffice.

This list of MoS groups may not be exhaustive, and not every AI algorithm will require metrics associated with every group. However, based on current literature, strategy, and technology, all MoS groups should be considered when developing metrics for AI solutions, and a reason should be given for any omission. We now discuss each group in more detail.

Reliability comprises mission reliability, system reliability, and algorithm reliability. Reliability in general refers to whether a system can be counted on to work as intended. Mission reliability refers to the likelihood that a solution will work sufficiently well to allow completion of a particular mission, while system reliability is essentially a measure of uptime. Algorithm reliability, while arguably a subset of system reliability, deserves separate mention because of the difference between ML code and traditional code:

> Unlike traditional code, which is written line by line in a sequential pattern (even if auto-generation is used), ML will be deployed as models, created by frameworks that learn. Models will, in a very real sense, be birthed. And like any form of offspring, you

---

[21] Public-Private Analytic Exchange Program, *AI: Using Standards to Mitigate Risks*, Washington, D.C.: U.S. Department of Homeland Security, 2018.

Table 5.4
Measures of Suitability

Group	Definitions
Reliability	*Mission reliability.* The probability of a system completing an attempted mission successfully, which depends on both the reliability of the hardware and the redundancy built into the system.[a]
	System reliability. The probability that an item will perform a required function without failure under stated conditions for a stated period.[b]
	Algorithm reliability. Behaving as expected, even for novel inputs.[c]
Maintainability/ sustainability	*Maintainability.* The ability of an item to be retained in, or restored to, a specified condition when maintenance is performed by personnel having specified skill levels, using prescribed procedures and resources, at each prescribed level of maintenance and repair.[d]
	Sustainability. The ability to maintain the necessary level and duration of operational activity to achieve military objectives. Sustainability is a function of providing for and maintaining those levels of ready forces, materiel and consumables necessary to support military effort.[d]
Interoperability	The ability of systems, units, or forces to provide data, information, materiel, and services to and accept the same from other systems, units, or forces and to use the data, information, materiel, and services so exchanged to enable them to operate effectively together.[e]
Scalability	The ability of a system, component, or process to "handle throughput changes roughly in proportion to the change in the number of units of or size of the inputs."[f]
Cybersecurity	Prevention of damage to, protection of, and restoration of computers, electronic communications systems, electronic communications services, wire communication, and electronic communication, including information contained therein, to ensure its availability, integrity, authentication, confidentiality, and nonrepudiation.[d]
Human-machine teaming	Human system integration is concerned with ensuring that the characteristics of people are considered throughout the system development process regarding their selection and training, their participation in system operation, and their health and safety. It is also concerned with providing tools and methods meeting these same requirements to support the system development process itself.[g]
Explainability/ credibility	The ability of an AI solution to explain the logic behind a recommendation or action, the ability to understand the logic behind recommendations, at least in the near term.[h]

[a] William L. Stanley and John L. Birkler, "Improvising Operational Suitability Through Better Requirements and Testing," R-3333-AF, a project AIR FORCE report prepared for the United States Air Force, November 1986.

[b] Memorandum of Agreement on Multi-Service Operational Test and Evaluation (MOT&E) and Operational Suitability Terminology and Definitions, February 2017; O'Connor and Kleyner, 2012.

[c] Steve Eglash, "Progress Toward Safe and Reliable AI," Stanford AI Lab Blog, May 2, 2019.

[d] Defense Acquisitions University, "Department of Defense Acquisition University (DAU) Foundational Learning Directorate Center for Acquisition and Program Management Fort Belvoir, Virginia," DAU Glossary of Defense Acquisition Acronyms and Terms, website.

[e] MOT&E, 2017.

[f] Linux Information Project, "Scalable Definition," undated.

[g] National Research Council, *Human-System Integration in the System Development Process: A New Look*, Washington, DC: The National Academies Press, 2007.

[h] DIB, *AI Principles: Recommendations on the Ethical Use of Artificial Intelligence by the Department of Defense*, Arlington, Va., 2019.

can never really be sure of just what you will be getting until it arrives.[22]

Reliability is particularly important for the responsible and effective use of AI: unreliable systems are prone to behavior outside the intended domain of use. As the Defense Innovation Board (DIB) put it:

> DoD AI systems should have an explicit, well-defined domain of use, and the safety, security, and robustness of such systems should be tested and assured across their entire life cycle within that domain of use.[23]

Maintainability and *sustainability* are important characteristics of any system. We group them together here because, while they are distinct for hardware, the difference between them is largely immaterial for software. For AI, however, there is a special flavor concerning the ability to maintain the necessary models and data: "Maintaining accurate model parameters requires that attention be given to the process by which the parameters are chosen and changed. [DoD] also needs to ensure that it will have the full sources of all of the models and data available for its use."[24]

Interoperability focuses on the AI system's ability to interact with existing systems. Interoperability is as important to AI solutions as it is to any other defense system. DIB emphasizes the need to consider interoperability in the testing and validation of defense systems:

> DoD should take care during T&E [test and evaluation] and V&V to adequately consider the overarching AI system of systems, including the interaction of subordinate, layered systems, and identification of and solutions to failure in one or more of

---

[22] Steve Roddy, "The Success of Machine Learning Rests on Scalability," *Massachusetts Institute of Technology Review*, November 14, 2019.

[23] DIB, 2019. See also Greg Zacharias, *Emerging Technologies: Test and Evaluation Implications*, Washington, D.C.: U.S. Department of Defense, April 10, 2019b.

[24] Defense Science Board, 2016.

the subsystems. This may in fact be impossible, given the inability to test, model, or simulate such a large state space, as well as adequately test all components in dynamic, unpredictable, and unstructured environments with high fidelity.[25]

Scalability is the ability to continue to function as expected when the requirements placed on an algorithm are raised. Curiously, scalability is not discussed much in strategic guidance documents or standard acquisition documents. This may be because the scale of use is generally specified in acquisition requirements. Nevertheless, we call out scalability as a particular concern for AI solutions because moving AI from the laboratory to large-scale use poses unique difficulties for training and testing:

> Communication time starts dominating total compute time as we parallelize to large-scale. . . . Therefore, we need to go beyond naïve parallelization schemes to be able to benefit from large computation resources (as in a public cloud) for reducing the time to train large models.[26]

Cybersecurity metrics address the "safety and security" issues raised in the strategic guidance documents, namely, maintaining the AI system's integrity. AI systems are vulnerable to attack, which could result in reduced performance or, in some instances, benefit an adversary. As noted by the National Science and Technology Council:

> AI systems also have their own cybersecurity needs. AI-driven applications should implement sound cybersecurity controls to ensure integrity of data and functionality, protect privacy and confidentiality, and maintain availability.[27]

---

[25] DIB, 2019. See also Zacharias, 2019b.

[26] Pradeep Dubey and Amir Khosrowshahi, "Scaling to Meet the Growing Needs of AI," Intel AI Developer Program, October 26, 2016.

[27] National Science and Technology Council Committee on Technology, *Preparing for the Future of Artificial Intelligence*, Washington, D.C.: Executive Office of the President, October 2016.

Human-machine teaming is an important aspect of integrating AI into the military context. AI systems may be implemented as fully autonomous, as human-on-the-loop systems, or as human-in-the-loop systems. Even when fully autonomous, however, AI systems will still be part of the larger human military effort. The proper choice of human-machine teaming takes advantage of both human and machine strengths:

> While completely autonomous AI systems will be important in some application domains, many other application areas (e.g., disaster recovery and medical diagnostics) are most effectively addressed by a combination of humans and AI systems working together to achieve application goals.[28]

We include training and testing with humans in this category. As a prior RAND study noted: "If the human is to be an integral part of the system tested, then the tests need to include the human to replicate real-world conditions."[29]

Explainability/credibility is the most discussed characteristic of AI systems in strategic guidance documents, and it also appears often in the academic literature. For example, Robert Hoffman and his coauthors identify several classes of explainability measures.[30] These measures may be resolved through user evaluations (e.g., surveys) after interacting with the AI.

The purpose of explainability is to offer credibility and trust. Having an explanation for why an AI system made a certain determination helps the user decide whether to accept or reject that result during the V&V process. Otherwise, AI appears to be a "black box." Explainability is commonly thought to be a prerequisite for trust:

---

[28] Select Committee on Artificial Intelligence, *The National Artificial Intelligence Research and Development Strategic Plan: 2019 Update*, Washington, D.C.: National Science and Technology Council, June 2019.

[29] Amado Cordova, Lindsay D. Millard, Lance Menthe, Robert A. Guffey, and Carl Rhodes, *Motion Imagery Processing and Exploitation (MIPE)*, Santa Monica, Calif.: RAND Corporation, RR-154-AF, 2013.

[30] For example, see Robert R. Hoffman, Shane T. Mueller, Gary Klein, and Jordan Litman, *Metrics for Explainable AI: Challenges and Prospects*, Ithaca, N.Y.: Cornell University, eprint arXiv:1812.04608, December 2018.

Truly trustworthy AI requires explainable AI, especially as AI systems grow in scale and complexity; this requires a comprehensive understanding of the AI system by the human user and the human designer.[31]

Analysis of Metric Categorization

As noted in Volume 2, the literature shows significant variation in the level of acceptance and interest in these categories. To determine whether these categories are relevant, we collected 241 metrics from 30 different DARPA Broad Agency Announcements, from the period 2014–2020, and assessed which category each metric belonged to, if any.[32] Figure 5.1 (top) shows the assignment of metrics to categories (including all categories discussed above), and Figure 5.1 (bottom) shows the percentage of programs with *at least* one metric per category.

Summary

In this chapter, we identified categories to guide the development of MoP, MoE, and MoS. We demonstrated that these were reasonable categories that appear to cover the range currently in use—but we also showed that there is a strong focus on MoP at the expense of the other two categories. Because all three categories are needed to evaluate the suitability of AI solutions to C2 problems in their operational context, we find three shortfalls in current practice:

1. *Too little focus on MoE and MoS.* Our review of DARPA metrics shows that the primary focus of AI evaluation tends to be on performance accuracy and optimality. While this is certainly important, this keeps the focus on the solution space. Strate-

---

[31] Select Committee on Artificial Intelligence, 2019.

[32] We originally considered 53 Broad Agency Announcements but narrowed it to 30 that were relevant to AI. Of the 258 metrics in these programs, 17 were judged not to be associated with AI, leaving 241 metrics. Two team members categorized all metrics separately and then reconciled their lists. There was initially a wide discrepancy in coding between the two members, which underscores the importance of clear definitions.

Figure 5.1
Defense Advanced Research Projects Agency Metric Classifications by Number (top) and by Percentage of Programs with Metric (bottom)

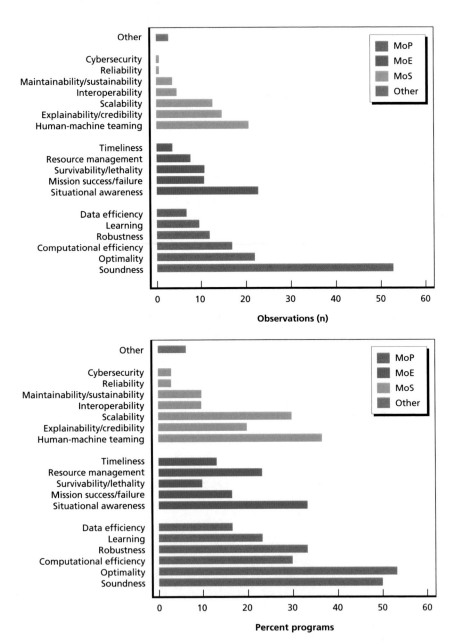

gic guidance documents indicate that equal consideration needs to be given to the problem space and to integration issues. An accurate and efficient algorithm is not of military utility if it is not addressing the right problem.

2. *Too little focus on data set availability and quality.* It is important to understand the limitations of the data being used to train and test the algorithm. As seen in our analysis of C2 problems, data set limitations are ubiquitous. The size and completeness of examples contained in a data set may dictate the use of additional methods to better train the model. Data sets may also benefit from their own data quality metrics to ensure minimal bias, balance, relevancy, sufficiency, currency, balance, and so on. The other side of this coin is better data may be more important to the results than a smarter algorithm.[33]

3. *Limited resources for evaluation of the impact of AI algorithms.* DIB plainly states that "DoD lacks AI T&E tools for validation of AI/ML models."[34] MoE and MoS require an operationally realistic environment in which the system can be tested. The focus on MoP may be partly responsible for obscuring these needs.

---

[33] For example, see Lance Menthe, Dahlia Anne Goldfeld, Abbie Tingstad, Sherrill Lingel, Edward Geist, Donald Brunk, Amanda Wicker, Sarah Soliman, Balys Gintautas, Anne Stickells, and Amado Cordova, *Technology Innovation and the Future of Air Force Intelligence Analysis*, Vol. 1, *Findings and Recommendations*, Santa Monica, Calif.: RAND Corporation, RR-A341-1, 2021.

[34] DIB, 2019.

Conclusion and Recommendations

To examine opportunities for applying AI to the military, we developed a structured method for (1) analyzing the characteristics of a given C2 process, (2) analyzing the capabilities of one or more AI systems, and (3) determining the suitability of an AI system for a given C2 process (Figure 6.1). The method can help identify the most promising AI systems for a given C2 process and guide the T&E of those systems once implemented.

In addition to providing a methodology to determine alignment between C2 problems and AI solutions, this research supports several conclusions shown in Figure 6.1 along with associated recommendations.

Conclusion 1. Command and Control Processes Are Very Different From Many of the Games and Environments Used to Develop and Demonstrate Artificial Intelligence Systems

Games such as chess, go, and even *StarCraft II* are qualitatively different from most real-world tasks. These games have well-defined rules (even if some of them are hidden from the player) that remain constant over time. Game-playing algorithms exploit this regularity to achieve superhuman performance. Unfortunately, nature and the adversary intervene to break this simplifying assumption in military tasks.

- *Recommendation 1.* Use the structured method described in this report to systematically analyze the characteristics of games,

Figure 6.1
Artificial Intelligence System Capability Mapping and Command and Control Process Evaluation

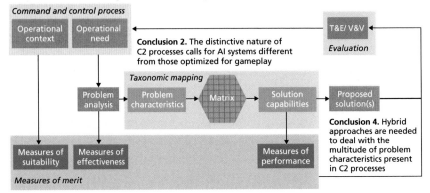

Conclusion 1. C2 processes are very different from many of the games and environments used to develop and demonstrate AI systems

Conclusion 2. The distinctive nature of C2 processes calls for AI systems different from those optimized for gameplay

Conclusion 4. Hybrid approaches are needed to deal with the multitude of problem characteristics present in C2 processes

Conclusion 3. New guidance, infrastructure, and metrics are needed to evaluate applications of AI to C2

problems, and C2 processes to determine where existing AI test beds are representative and nonrepresentative of C2 tasks.

- *Recommendation 2.* Develop new AI test beds with problem characteristics that are representative of C2 tasks in kind and in intensity.
- Characterizing and developing representative problems and environments will enable research, development, test, and evaluation of AI systems under conditions representative of DoD problem sets, thereby increasing transferability to operational environments. Additionally, it will enable direct comparison of disparate AI systems to one another.

Conclusion 2. The Distinctive Nature of Command and Control Processes Calls For Artificial Intelligence Systems Different From Those Optimized For Game Play

Algorithms optimized for playing games, such as alpha-beta pruning and AlphaZero, are not easily adapted to most C2 tasks. Games and

C2 problems are qualitatively different, and they demand qualitatively different algorithms. Fortunately, there are algorithms such as width-based planners that appear to be a promising fit for at least some challenging C2 problems.

- *Recommendation 3.* Use the structured method described in this report to identify and invest in high-priority solution capabilities called for across a wide range of C2 processes and not currently available (e.g., robustness and assuredness).
- *Recommendation 4.* Use the structured method described in this report to evaluate alignment between the characteristics of potential AI systems and particular C2 processes to prioritize which systems to develop.

Understanding the capabilities and limitations of existing AI systems will allow the Air Force to identify systems that are suitable for different C2 processes a priori. Choosing the right approach at problem outset can substantially reduce application development time, increase solution quality, and decrease risk associated with transitioning the solution.

Conclusion 3. New Guidance, Infrastructure, and Metrics Are Needed to Evaluate Applications of Artificial Intelligence to Command and Control

AI systems are typically evaluated using a limited set of measures of performance, such as accuracy and optimality; however, other system capabilities like timeliness and robustness may be equally important. Additionally, because AI is intended as a component of larger C2 architectures, measures of performance alone do not enable comprehensive assessment. Additional measures of effectiveness and suitability are needed to evaluate the AI system in the context of the C2 architecture.

- *Recommendation 5.* Develop metrics for AI solutions that assess capabilities beyond algorithm soundness and optimality (e.g., robustness and explainability).

- *Recommendation 6.* Use the structured method described in this report to identify key measures of performance, effectiveness, and suitability for a given C2 process.
- *Recommendation 7.* Perform a comprehensive assessment of AI systems for a given C2 process based on identified measures of merit.

Establishing and operationalizing measures of merit will enable the evaluation and comparison of potential AI systems. Additionally, measures of merit provide a way to communicate the return on investment of AI-enabled C2.

Conclusion 4. Hybrid Approaches Are Needed to Deal With the Multitude of Problem Characteristics Present In Command and Control Processes

Problem characteristics call for multiple solution capabilities, some of which are hard to achieve together. Volume 2 contains three technical case studies that demonstrate a wide range of computational, AI, and human solutions to various C2 problems.

The first case study compared two computational approaches for developing the MAAP—a MIP and a greedy heuristic. The MIP increased plan quality whereas the heuristic increased planning speed. Yet a hybrid solution that combined the heuristic and the MIP was more suitable for developing the MAAP than either of the parts alone.

The second case study compared two architectures for performing airborne target recognition—one that used reinforcement learning alone and one that used reinforcement learning along with recommendations from an expert system. Of the two architectures, only the hybrid one was robust against sensor noise.

The third case study examined a mixed-initiative system for personnel recovery. The complexity of the state space resisted a complete human solution whereas the shortage of historical or simulator data resisted a complete AI solution. A hybrid solution that combined human knowledge with optimal Bayesian updating by a machine was most suitable for personnel recovery.

The main conclusion from these case studies is that hybrid approaches are often needed to deal with the range of characteristics present in C2 problems.

- *Recommendation 8.* Identify, reuse, and combine algorithmic solutions that confer critical AI system capabilities.

Throughout this report, we focused on AI for Air Force C2. However, given the generality of the analytical framework and the emergence of JADC2, all these conclusions and recommendations extend to the pursuit of AI across DoD.

References

Air Force Life Cycle Management Center, Battle Management Directorate, *Descriptive List of Applicable Publications (DLOAP) for the Air Operations Center (AOC)*, Hanscom Air Force Base, Mass., April 1, 2019. Not available to the general public.

Alberts, David S., and Richard E. Hayes, *Understanding Command and Control*, Washington, D.C.: Command and Control Research Program, 2006.

Anderson, J. R., *Cognitive Psychology and Its Implications*, New York: Macmillan, 2005.

Arbel, T., and F. P. Ferrie, "On the Sequential Accumulation of Evidence," *International Journal of Computer Vision*, Vol. 43, 2001, pp. 205–230.

Army Doctrine Publication 6-0, *Mission Command: Command and Control of Army Forces*, Washington, D.C.: U.S. Department of the Army, 2019.

Askham, Nicola, Denise Cook, Martin Doyle, Helen Fereday, Mike Gibson, Ulrich Landbeck, Rob Lee, Chris Maynard, Gary Palmer, and Julian Schwarzenbach, *The Six Primary Dimensions for Data Quality Assessment: Data Quality Dimensions*, Bristol, U.K.: Data Management Association and Data Quality Dimensions Working Group, October 2013.

Boyd, John R., "Patterns of Conflict," unpublished briefing slides, 1986.

Brown, N., and T. Sandholm, "Superhuman AI for Heads-Up No-Limit Poker: Libratus Beats Top Professionals," *Science*, Vol. 359, No. 6374, 2018, pp. 418–424.

Cordova, Amado, Lindsay D. Millard, Lance Menthe, Robert A. Guffey, and Carl Rhodes, *Motion Imagery Processing and Exploitation (MIPE)*, Santa Monica, Calif.: RAND Corporation, RR-154-AF, 2013. As of December 15, 2020: https://www.rand.org/pubs/research_reports/RR154.html

Dahm, W. J., *Technology Horizons: A Vision for Air Force Science and Technology During 2010–2030*, Arlington, Va.: U.S. Air Force, 2010.

DARPA—*See* Defense Advanced Research Projects Agency.

Defense Acquisitions University, "Department of Defense Acquisition University (DAU) Foundational Learning Directorate Center for Acquisition and Program Management Fort Belvoir, Virginia," DAU Glossary of Defense Acquisition Acronyms and Terms, website. As of January 7, 2020: https://www.dau.edu/glossary/Pages/Glossary.aspx

Defense Advanced Research Projects Agency, "DARPA Announces $2 Billion Campaign to Develop Next Wave of AI Technologies," Arlington, Va., March 12, 2020. As of March 23, 2020: https://www.darpa.mil/news-events/2018-09-07

Defense Innovation Board, *AI Principles: Recommendations on the Ethical Use of Artificial Intelligence by the Department of Defense*, Arlington, Va., 2019.

Defense Science Board, *Defense Science Board Summer Study on Autonomy*, Washington, D.C.: Office of the Under Secretary of Defense, June 2016.

DIB—*See* Defense Innovation Board.

DoD—*See* U.S. Department of Defense.

Dubey, Pradeep, and Amir Khosrowshahi, "Scaling to Meet the Growing Needs of AI," Intel AI Developer Program, October 26, 2016. As of March 20, 2020: https://software.intel.com/en-us/articles/scaling-to-meet-the-growing-needs-of-ai

Dulac-Arnold, Gabriel, Daniel Mankowitz, and Todd Hester, *Challenges of Real-World Reinforcement Learning*, Ithaca, N.Y.: Cornell University, eprint arXiv:1904.12901, April 2019. As of December 22, 2020: https://arxiv.org/abs/1904.12901

Eglash, Steve, "Progress Toward Safe and Reliable AI," Stanford AI Lab Blog, May 2, 2019. As of December 22, 2020: http://ai.stanford.edu/blog/reliable-ai/

Ensmenger, N., "Is Chess the Drosophila of Artificial Intelligence? A Social History of an Algorithm," *Social Studies of Science*, Vol. 42, No. 1, 2012, pp. 5–30.

Endsley, Mica R., "Design and Evaluation for Situation Awareness Enhancement," *Proceedings of the Human Factors Society Annual Meeting*, Vol. 32, No. 2, 1988, pp. 97–101. As of March 19, 2020: https://journals.sagepub.com/doi/pdf/10.1177/154193128803200221

Fitch, Kathryn, Steven J. Bernstein, Maria Dolores Aguilar, Bernard Burnand, Juan Ramon LaCalle, Pablo Lazaro, Mirjam van het Loo, Joseph McDonnell, Janneke Vader, and James P. Kahan, *The RAND/UCLA Appropriateness Method User's Manual*, Santa Monica, Calif.: RAND Corporation, MR-1269-DG-XII/RE, 2001. As of December 15, 2020: https://www.rand.org/pubs/monograph_reports/MR1269.html

Gobet, F., and H. A. Simon, "Templates in Chess Memory: A Mechanism for Recalling Several Boards," *Cognitive Psychology*, Vol. 31, No. 1, 1996, pp. 1–40.

Hannun, A. Y., P. Rajpurkar, M. Haghpanahi, G. H. Tison, C. Bourn, M. P. Turakhia, and A. Y. Ng, "Cardiologist-Level Arrhythmia Detection and Classification in Ambulatory Electrocardiograms Using a Deep Neural Network," *Nature Medicine*, Vol. 25, No. 1, 2019, p. 65.

Hoffman, Robert R., Shane T. Mueller, Gary Klein, and Jordan Litman, *Metrics for Explainable AI: Challenges and Prospects*, Ithaca, N.Y.: Cornell University, eprint arXiv:1812.04608, December 2018. As of December 22, 2020: https://arxiv.org/abs/1812.04608

Jamei, Mahdi, Letif Mones, Alex Robson, Lyndon White, James Requeima, and Cozmin Ududec, *Meta-Optimization of Optimal Power Flow*, International Conference on Machine Learning, Climate Change: How Can AI Help, Long Beach, Calif., 2019.

Joint Publication 3-0, *Joint Operations*, Washington, D.C.: U.S. Joint Chiefs of Staff, January 17, 2017.

———, *Command and Control of Joint Air Operations*, Washington, D.C.: U.S. Joint Chiefs of Staff, January 12, 2010.

Julian, K. D., M. J. Kochenderfer, and M. P. Owen, "Deep Neural Network Compression for Aircraft Collision Avoidance Systems," *Journal of Guidance, Control, and Dynamics*, Vol. 42, No. 3, 2019, pp. 598–608.

Khodyakov, D., S. Grant, B. Denger, K. Kinnett, A. Martin, M. Booth, C. Armstrong, E. Dao, C. Chen, I. Coulter, H. Peay, G. Hazlewood, and N. Street, "Using an Online, Modified Delphi Approach to Engage Patients and Caregivers in Determining the Patient-Centeredness of Duchenne Muscular Dystrophy Care Considerations," *Medical Decision Making*, Vol. 39, No. 8, 2019, pp. 1019–1031.

Linux Information Project, "Scalable Definition," undated. As of December 22, 2020: http://www.linfo.org/scalable.html

Lockheed Martin Information Systems and Global Services, *Technical Requirements Document (TRD), for the Air and Space Operations Center (AOC) Weapon System (WS)*, draft, AOCWS-TRD-0000-U-R8C0, prepared for 652 ELSS/KQ Electronic Systems Center, Hanscom AFB, Colorado Springs, Colo.: Lockheed Martin Information Systems and Global Services, November 16, 2009. Not available to the general public.

Marr, Bernard, and Matt Ward, *Artificial Intelligence in Practice: How 50 Successful Companies Used AI and Machine Learning to Solve Problems*, Chichester, U.K.: Wiley, 2019.

McKinsey Global Institute, Jacques Bughin, Eric Hazan, Sree Ramaswamy, Michael Chui, Tera Allas, Peter Dahlström, Nicolaus Henke, and Monica Trench, *Artificial Intelligence: The Next Digital Frontier?*, New York: McKinsey & Company, June 2017.

Memorandum of Agreement on Multi-Service Operational Test and Evaluation (MOT&E) and Operational Suitability Terminology and Definitions, February 2017.

Menthe, Lance, Dahlia Anne Goldfeld, Abbie Tingstad, Sherrill Lingel, Edward Geist, Donald Brunk, Amanda Wicker, Sarah Soliman, Balys Gintautas, Anne Stickells, and Amado Cordova, *Technology Innovation and the Future of Air Force Intelligence Analysis*, Vol. 1, *Findings and Recommendations*, Santa Monica, Calif.: RAND Corporation, RR-A341-1, 2021. As of January 27, 2021: https://www.rand.org/pubs/research_reports/RRA341-1.html

Mnih, Volodymyr, Koray Kavukcuoglu, David Silver, Alex Graves, Ioannis Antonoglou, Daan Wierstra, and Martin Riedmiller, *Playing Atari with Deep Reinforcement Learning*, Ithaca, N.Y., Cornell University, eprint arXiv:1312.5602, December 2013. As of December 22, 2020: https://arxiv.org/abs/1312.5602

National Research Council, *Funding a Revolution: Government Support for Computing Research*, Washington, D.C.: National Academy Press, 1999.

———, *Human-System Integration in the System Development Process: A New Look*, Washington, DC: The National Academies Press, 2007.

National Science and Technology Council Committee on Technology, *Preparing for the Future of Artificial Intelligence*, Washington, D.C.: Executive Office of the President, October 2016.

National Security Commission on Artificial Intelligence, *Interim Report*, Arlington, Va., 2019.

North Atlantic Treaty Organization, *Code of Best Practice for C2 Assessment*, Brussels: Research and Technology Organization, 2002.

Public-Private Analytic Exchange Program, *AI: Using Standards to Mitigate Risks*, Washington, D.C.: U.S. Department of Homeland Security, 2018. As of March 20, 2020: https://www.dhs.gov/sites/default/files/publications/2018_AEP_Artificial _Intelligence.pdf

Reich, Y., and A. Kapeliuk, "A Framework for Organizing the Space of Decision Problems with Application to Solving Subjective, Context-Dependent Problems," *Decision Support Systems*, Vol. 41, No. 1, 2005, pp. 1–19.

Rittle, H. W. J., and M. M. Webber, "Dilemmas in a General Theory of Planning," *Policy Sciences*, Vol. 4, No. 2, 1973, pp. 155–169.

Roddy, Steve, "The Success of Machine Learning Rests on Scalability," *Massachusetts Institute of Technology Review*, November 14, 2019. As of March 20, 2020: https://www.technologyreview.com/s/614660/the-success-of-machine-learning -rests-on-scalability/

Russell, S., and P. Norvig, *Introduction to Artificial Intelligence: A Modern Approach*, New Delhi: Prentice-Hall of India, 1995.

Select Committee on Artificial Intelligence, *The National Artificial Intelligence Research and Development Strategic Plan: 2019 Update*, Washington, D.C.: National Science and Technology Council, June 2019.

Shanahan, John, "Artificial Intelligence Initiatives," statement to the Senate Armed Services Committee Subcommittee on Emerging Threats and Capabilities, Washington, D.C., U.S. Senate, March 12, 2019.

Silver, David, Thomas Hubert, Julian Schrittwieser, Ioannis Antonoglou, Matthew Lai, Arthur Guez, Marc Lanctot, Laurent Sifre, Dharshan Kumaran, Thore Graepel, Timothy Lillicrap, Karen Simonyan, and Demis Hassabi, "A General Reinforcement Learning Algorithm that Masters Chess, Shogi, and Go Through Self-Play," *Science*, Vol. 362, No. 6419, December 2018, pp. 1–32. As of March 23, 2020:
https://science.sciencemag.org/content/362/6419/1140

Sinha, Arunesh, Fei Fang, Bo An, Christopher Kiekintveld, and Milind Tambe, "Stackelberg Security Games: Looking Beyond a Decade of Success," *Proceedings of the International Joint Conferences on Artificial Intelligence*, Vienna: IJCAI, 2018, pp. 5494–5501.

Stanley William L., and John L. Birkler, "Improvising Operational Suitability Through Better Requirements and Testing," R-3333-AF, a project AIR FORCE report prepared for the United States Air Force, November 1986.

Strout, Nathan, "The 3 Major Security Threats to AI," C4ISRNET, September 10, 2019. As of March 20, 2020:
https://www.c4isrnet.com/artificial-intelligence/2019/09/10/the-3-major-security -threats-to-ai/

Tingstad, Abbie, Dahlia Anne Goldfeld, Lance Menthe, Robert A. Guffey, Zachary Haldeman, Krista S. Langeland, Amado Cordova, Elizabeth M. Waina, and Balys Gintautas, *Assessing the Value of Intelligence Collected by U.S. Air Force Airborne Intelligence, Surveillance, and Reconnaissance Platforms*, Santa Monica, Calif.: RAND Corporation, RR-2742-AF, 2021. As of June 15, 2021:
https://www.rand.org/pubs/research_reports/RR2742.html

U.S. Air Force, *Artificial Intelligence Annex to the Department of Defense Artificial Intelligence Strategy*, Washington, D.C., 2019a.

———, *Science and Technology Strategy: Strengthening USAF Science and Technology for 2030 and Beyond*, Washington, D.C., April 2019b.

U.S. Air Force Doctrine, *Annex 3-30: Command and Control*, Maxwell Air Force Base, Ala.: Lemay Center for Doctrine, 2020.

U.S. Air Force Scientific Advisory Board, *Technologies for Enabling Resilient Command and Control MDC2 Overview*, Washington, D.C., 2018.

U.S. Department of Defense, *A Critical Change to the Air Operations Center— Weapon System Increment 10.2 Program Increased Costs and Delayed Deployment for 3 Years*, Washington, D.C.: Inspector General, DODIG-2017-079, 2017a.

————, *Glossary of Defense Acquisition Acronyms and Terms*, Fort Belvoir, Va.: Defense Acquisition University, 2017b.

————, *Artificial Intelligence Strategy*, Washington, D.C., 2018.

————, "Secretary of Defense Speech: Reagan National Defense Forum Keynote," Defense.gov, December 7, 2019. As of December 22, 2020:
https://www.defense.gov/Newsroom/Speeches/Speech/Article/2035046/reagan
-national-defense-forum-keynote-remarks/

U.S. Marine Corps, *Command and Control*, Doctrinal Publication 6, Washington, D.C., 2018.

Vinyals, Oriol, Igor Babuschkin, Wojciech M. Czarnecki, et al., "Grandmaster Level in Starcraft II Using Multi-Agent Reinforcement Learning," *Nature*, Vol. 575, No. 7782, 2019, pp. 350–354.

Wagstaff, Kri L., "Machine Learning that Matters," *Proceedings of the 29th International Conference on Machine Learning*, Madison, Wisc.: Omnipress, 2012, pp. 529–536.

Walch, Kathleen, "Are We Heading for Another AI Winter Soon?," *Forbes*, October 20, 2019. As of December 22, 2020:
https://www.forbes.com/sites/cognitiveworld/2019/10/20/are-we-heading-for
-another-ai-winter-soon/?sh=7fbdfba156d6

Winkler, Robert, *The Evolution of the Joint ATO Cycle*, Norfolk, Va.: Joint Advanced Warfighting School, 2006.

Wong, Yuna Huh, John M. Yurchak, Robert W. Button, Aaron Frank, Burgess Laird, Osonde A. Osoba, Randall Steeb, Benjamin N. Harris, and Sebastian Joon Bae, *Deterrence in the Age of Thinking Machines*, Santa Monica, Calif.: RAND Corporation, RR-2797-RC, 2020. As of December 22, 2020:
https://www.rand.org/pubs/research_reports/RR2797.html

Zacharias, Greg, *Autonomous Horizons: The Way Forward*, Maxwell Air Force Base, Ala.: Air University Press, Curtis E. LeMay Center for Doctrine Development and Education, 2019a.

————, *Emerging Technologies: Test and Evaluation Implications*, Washington, D.C.: U.S. Department of Defense, April 10, 2019b.